MW00465294

Content-Area Writing That ROCKS

and Works!

Rebecca G. Harper, Ph.D.

Publishing Credits

Corinne Burton, M.A.Ed., *President;* Conni Medina, M.A.Ed., *Managing Editor;*
Nika Fabienke, Ed.D., *Content Director;* Angela Johnson-Rogers, M.F.A., M.S.Ed., *Editor;*
Lee Aucoin, *Senior Graphic Designer;* Valerie Morales, *Assistant Editor*

Image Credits

Photo Images are from iStock and Shutterstock. Classroom images are courtesy of Rebecca G. Harper.

Standards

© Copyright 2010. National Governors Association Center for Best Practices and Council of Chief State School Officers. All rights reserved.

Shell Education

A division of Teacher Created Materials
5301 Oceanus Drive
Huntington Beach, CA 92649-1030

http://www.tcmpub.com/shell-education

ISBN 978-1-4258-1650-6

©2017 Shell Education Publishing, Inc.

The classroom teacher may reproduce copies of materials in this book for classroom use only. The reproduction of any part for an entire school or school system is strictly prohibited. No part of this publication may be transmitted, stored, or recorded in any form without written permission from the publisher.

Table of Contents

Dedication 5

Acknowledgments **6**

Why Writing? 7
    Organization of This Book 10

Content-Area Literacy and Writing 12
    The Importance of Content-Area Writing 12
    Reading and Writing Are Social Activities 13
    Students at the Center 14
    Embracing the Process 15
    How Does Content-Area Writing Look? 15
    How Do I Infuse My Content-Area Lessons with Writing? 18
    Making Content-Area Writing Work for All Learners 20

Writing to Think 23
        Who's the Writing For? 25
        Writing-to-Think Strategies 25
        Written Conversations 27
        Writing Breaks 30
        Dialogue Journals 33

Writing to Prove 36
        Paint-Strip Evidence 38
        Red-Light, Green-Light Evidence 40
        Textual-Evidence Throw Down 42
        Picture This! 45
        Do This, Not That Recipe 47
        Create a Simile 49
        Continuum Debate 51
        iPod® List 53

Writing to Learn Vocabulary 55
  Levels of Words 57
  Paint-Strip Words 59
  Continuum of Words 61
  Alpha-Boxes 63
  Also Known As (AKA) 66

Writing to Summarize 68
  Postcard Summaries 69
  Sports Summaries 71
  Trailers, Recaps, and Reviews 73
  Five-Dollar Summaries 75
  Comic-Strip Summaries 77
  Bio Poems 2.0 79
  Social Media Summaries 81

Writing to Organize 85
  Four-Block Writing 86
  Paint-Strip Organizer 89
  Heard, Refute, and Question (HRQ) 91
  List, Group, Label, and Map 93
  Compare-and-Contrast Throw Down 95
  Mock Pinterest Pages 99

Appendices 101
  Appendix A: Letter from the Author 101
  Appendix B: References Cited 102
  Appendix C: Interest Inventories 105
  Appendix D: Student Templates 108
  Appendix E: Books That Rock! 118

Dedication

For My Mother: Dr. Gayle S. Lee

(July 23, 1956–December 20, 2016)

Thank you for being a strong woman and for raising me to be one.

I will love you forever.

I miss you already.

Acknowledgments

Writing this book would never have happened without the help and support of my husband, Will, and our wonderful children, Amelia, Macy Belle, and Vin. You give me so much to be thankful for. I am one lucky woman. Thank you for loving me.

This book would not have been possible without the help of many of my students. While they all influenced me in some form or fashion, several were instrumental in helping me secure the needed sample photographs. Special thanks to:

Justin Boyington

Nicole Carpenter Caín

Amanda Hamilton

Karah Koellner

Alicia Stephenson

Brittany Reed

Jodi Wade

Also, thank you to my own children, Amelia and Macy Belle, who provided additional work samples. (Vin, we will catch you in the next book!)

And to all those friends, family members, students, and colleagues who supported and accepted me—feather boa, glitter, stilettos, and all—I thank you for believing in me before I did.

Why Writing?

According to the National Writing Project (2004), writing skills are among the most important skills needed to be successful. Most careers require individuals to possess at least rudimentary writing skills, and many include a need for job-specific writing skills. Writing serves as a vehicle for communication, a way to express ideas, and a way to respond to others. Being able to write, and write well, opens doors for people. It eliminates barriers caused by cultural and social differences as well as socioeconomic inequities.

The National Commission on Writing for America's Families, Schools, and Colleges (2004) states that "In today's workplace, writing is a 'threshold skill' for hiring and promotion among salaried (i.e., professional) employees. Survey results indicate that writing is a ticket to professional opportunity, while poorly written job applications are a figurative kiss of death" (3). Plus, writing serves as a gateway to "students' emerging role in our nation's future as participants and decision makers in a democratic society" (National Writing Project and Nagin 2006).

Today's students must know how to write for a variety of purposes and audiences. Modern classrooms around the world have already begun integrating college and career readiness standards into their curriculum. These standards emphasize the multifaceted nature of writing and the need to demonstrate competency in composition for a variety of purposes and audiences. To achieve this, students should write daily, both inside and outside school.

The good news is that many people, even students, write for a number of reasons on a daily basis—only the audience and formats morph and shift. If you ask a random person whether he or she has written something on a given day, he or she may say no at first. But upon reflection may realize that the volume of writing that he or she actually does in any given day is enormous. In most cases, people are not writing novels daily, but they are writing notes to themselves, messages to friends, and/or public statements, among other things. The progression of technology (smartphones, tablets, computers, etc.) brings even more reasons and ways to write daily.

Rock Star Tip

Have you written, anything today? Make a list of all of the things you've written, starting from when you woke up. You will be surprised how long the list is.

While grocery lists and text messages are not academic writing, bringing these kinds of writing activities into the classroom helps students begin to see that writing is more than creating essays. Students see that writers are not only those who write novels and plays but are people who do the following:

- ★ write blogs
- ★ write emails
- ★ write postcards
- ★ write to-do lists
- ★ write in journals

- ★ write text messages
- ★ write thank-you notes
- ★ take notes to prepare for a test
- ★ write posts and comment on social media

Part of the appeal of everyday informal writing and responding is its instantaneous nature. The writer is responding to his or her environment, sharing his/her life, and finding community. With the inclusion of social media, today's students are growing up with a constant audience of family, friends, and followers. The challenge for teachers is to guide students to understand that there can be a bridge between personal writing and academic, school-driven writing activities.

If students have opportunities for informal writing in their personal lives, and college and career readiness standards require more and more varied writing in Language Arts classes, what is the importance of content-area writing? Writing in the content areas provides students additional opportunities to share, learn, and explore content and practice writing mechanics. It also gives students an authentic space to practice writing in different genres and about different topics.

Think about it—writing the steps to solve computations in mathematics allows students to not only go back and revisit their solving process (explain their steps) but gives them practice writing instructional procedural texts. Using primary sources in social studies when completing document-based questions (DBQs) offers students a space to practice reading and using textual evidence to answer questions based on their reading. These two tasks are very different, but the skills employed by one task can benefit the other and ultimately strengthen students' overall writting ability. Each task, although content specific, has the potential to seep into other areas, offering students what we know they need: multiple, repeated opportunities to write.

Rock Star Tip

Remember, in order for students to understand the material, remember it, and use it, they must act on the information learned (Hyde 2006).

Content-area writing brings all the cognitive benefits of writing to science, social studies, math, and the arts. In fact, Langer and Applebee (1987) comment that the more the content is manipulated, the greater the potential for recall and understanding. Generally speaking, using written responses with reading increases student performance more than reading without the implementation of written tasks. Additionally, the ability and propensity to read and understand nonfiction (most of the text encountered in content-area classrooms) is a necessary skill for students involved in inquiry and research, making the act of writing across the curriculum a necessity to students' success outside the classroom (Harvey 1998).

Reading and writing are dependent on a common foundation of cognitive abilities that include visual, phonological, and semantic systems. A task or exercise that improves any of these foundational attributes could have implications on both reading and writing development (Berninger and Swanson 1994; Ellis 1985,1987; McCutchen 2000; Swanson and Berninger 1996).

Writing can be used as a tool for thinking, processing, learning, summarizing, organizing, and reflecting. Writing can be used to communicate ideas and thoughts, build a position for an argument, and keep you on track when you are at the grocery store. Writing is evolving and changing as technology advances and additional types of media become more common. Writing is versatile; it has unique properties that change depending on the objective. Most importantly, writing has the potential to improve learning. Combs advocated for writing instruction, concluding that "writing serves as a vehicle for learning both content standards and standards of written expression" (Combs 2012, 12). This is precisely why writing in the content-area classroom is absolutely necessary.

When implementing writing in the content-area classroom, consider what prior knowledge students bring to the task and content. Research indicates that students' knowledge about topics or concepts affects the writing quality and organizational nature of their written responses (Langer 1984; Newell and Winograd 1995).

Author's Thoughts

Part of my job as a professor of literacy is to show teachers how to incorporate literacy in their classrooms. Yet many of those I teach are not literacy teachers by trade. Their fields are unique, include diverse vocabulary exclusive to that area, and have subtle nuances and distinctions. In many instances, their training in literacy is limited to one or two basic courses taken early in their programs and careers. Imagine how a chemistry or an algebra teacher feels when he or she learns that the district is implementing reading and writing in all courses across all grade levels. Frustrated? Overwhelmed? Ticked off? He or she probably feels any one of those emotions—with good reason.

Some teachers are unsure of how their piece of the puzzle fits into the overall portrait of a literate student. How does literacy in chemistry add to, develop, and mold students into becoming literate individuals?

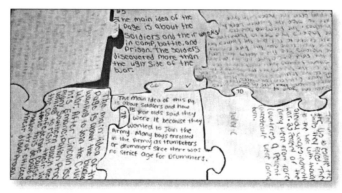

☆ Writing is a unique puzzle. Each teacher in your school functions as a piece in creating literate students.

© Shell Education

Organization of This Book

Each section of this book is devoted to an essential skill. Within the sections, peppered throughout the book, are several activities that can be used to teach each skill. They are a mix of background information, practical activities, useful tips, and fun anecdotes showcasing the activities used in a content-area lesson.

The *Content-Area Literacy and Writing* section gives an overview of the importance of and basis for content-area literacy.

The *Writing to Think* section presents strategies that employ writing as a tool for thinking and communicating. The strategies in this section can be used flexibly to prompt students to think and process information.

The Writing to Prove section focuses on writing strategies that use evidence to prove and support student thinking and learning. The strategies in this section require students to prove and support their opinions based on textual evidence, observations, and synthesizing conclusions drawn from classroom/life experiences.

The *Writing to Learn Vocabulary* section presents strategies to scaffold students' vocabulary acquisition in the content-area classroom. These strategies will be especially useful in subject-area lessons that depend on vocabulary acquisition to fully grasp subject-specific content.

The *Writing to Summarize* section offers creative suggestions to guide students to recap and condense material. Every classroom requires students to summarize. This section offers several social media strategies to pique students' interest.

The Writing to Organize section is just that—ways to integrate the crucial skill of organization into content-area writing instruction. Each strategy offers opportunities for compartmentalizing and organizing content for later use.

Note: Many strategies in this book, when differentiated, can serve multiple purposes and teach multiple skills. For example, while Dialogue Journals are in the *Writing to Think* section, this activity can also be modified to teach summarization in the *Writing to Summarize* section.

The Appendices provide activity templates, interest inventories that can be used during instruction, and a supplemental book list that can support the content-area classroom.

There are 26 skill-specific strategies in this book. Each strategy is structured similarly to a lesson plan to give a clear and organized snapshot of the writing activity. Each strategy starts with a background, procedure, and modification section to guide implementation. All activities conclude with extension ideas and a content-area crossover section. These sections are intended to be content-specific, giving the content-area teacher a set of differentiated ideas and modifications to meet the needs of all students in his or her classroom.

The *background* section explains the rationale for the strategy. Teachers will find an overall synopsis of the strategy along with any pertinent research.

Aside from teaching the overall skill, each strategy has additional *benefits* for students in the content-area classroom.

The *procedure* section is organized into quick and easy steps.

Each strategy offers *modifications* to best support diverse learners.

The *extensions* can be applied to extend the strategy and lengthen the writing activity.

Each lesson ends with a *content-area crossover*, which offers multiple suggestions for how the strategy can be adapted across the content area.

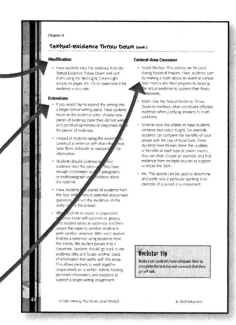

Content-Area Literacy and Writing

The Importance of Content-Area Writing

Many of my colleagues saw reading and writing across the curriculum initiatives as a help to the English Language Arts (ELA) teacher. It's important to note that it's not *just* ELA teachers who shoulder this responsibility. While any increase in writing certainly benefits ELA teachers, the biggest benefit goes to students who gain additional experience, exposure, and confidence in writing.

Just about every national content-area organization has advocated for more content-area writing in the classroom. In fact, the National Council of Teachers of Mathematics (NCTM), the National Science Teachers Association (NSTA), and the National Council for Social Studies (NCSS) all proclaim the importance and necessity of quality literacy strategies integrated in content areas. NCSS (2015) recently released a free Massive Open Online Course titled "Improving Historical Reading and Writing" on their website for teachers to use to improve skills in teaching historical literacy. NCTM's Principals and Standards for School Mathematics (2000) includes a communication strand for each grade band, which requires students to communicate their ideas both orally and in written formats, using the language of mathematics to express mathematical ideas precisely, generate explanations, formulate questions, write arguments, reflect on learning, and describe problem-solving strategies. NSTA's standards require students to formulate and construct arguments with appropriate evidence, explain and analyze scientific data, present data in a myriad of visual formats, develop questions, and hypothesize and synthesize complex information in a variety of written formats. In fact, according to the Next Generation Science Standards (2013, 1), "literacy skills are critical to building knowledge in science."

Drumming for More

Want to read more about literacy? Take a look at James Paul Gee's *"What Is Literacy?"* article.

Aside from the endorsement from content-area organizations, it is difficult to encounter a set of academic standards that does not emphasize content writing in some form. Most of the College and Career Readiness Standards are infused with literacy and emphasize literacy across disciplines, genres, and grade bands. The literacy skills vary in depth and skill level, emphasizing sophistication and complexity of content-area writing.

What exactly is content-area literacy? McKenna and Robinson (1990, 167) define it as "the ability to use reading and writing for the acquisition of new content in a given discipline. Such ability includes three principal cognitive components: general literacy skills, content-specific literacy skills, and prior knowledge of content."

Content-area literacy is not a substitute for content-area knowledge, and it does not take the place of knowing and understanding the complex network of standards used in each subject area. Similarly, it is not a substitute for explicit writing or literacy instruction that typically occurs in the ELA classroom. Instead, it is used to aid in the learning and acquisition of skills and material addressed in subject-area classrooms.

> ### Rock Star Tip
> Certain reading behaviors, such as skimming or scanning texts and close reading, can be employed in a variety of areas. Their purpose transcends subject areas and is not discipline specific.

Reading and Writing Are Social Activities

According to social learning theory, learning occurs through the day-to-day interactions and observations that individuals take part in and observe in everyday situations (Bandura 1977). Lankshear and Knobel (1998, 165) explain that "if learning is to be efficacious, then what a child or adult does now as a learner must be connected in meaningful and motivating ways with 'mature' (insider) versions of related social practices." In other words, connections between learning and practices that exist in social institutions outside of school should be meaningful and authentic.

Reading and writing are examples of "socially constructed phenomenon" (Cook-Gumperz 1986, 61). They are both social processes, influenced by the context and individual experiences of each reader and writer. The act of writing—the recording of pictorial images or words on a page—is a dynamic act, one that is codependent on the writer and the reader. Similarly, the act of reading involves recalling information, transacting with the text on a number of levels, and making associations with the text based on past experiences and cultural background (Rosenblatt 1994). Neither reading nor writing is a static transaction—it is dynamic and hinges on background knowledge, interpretation, and personal experiences and histories.

There are numerous writing strategies for the content-area classroom that capitalize on the social phenomena for writing. For example, the Written Conversations (page 27) and Dialogue Journals (page 33) activities have shown to be effective with both peers and teachers. Conversations of any type, including written ones, carve out a space in the class for students and teachers to talk about content, both in process and in product.

Acknowledging the social nature of writing is necessary for success, but it is equally important to recognize that each learner has unique needs and backgrounds. The learner uses these unique characteristics that are derived from cultural and historical influences to participate in school culture (Hollie 2012). Moll, Amanti, Neff, and Gonzalez (1992, 134) refer to this as "funds of knowledge." These funds of knowledge are historically and culturally collected information and wisdoms shared by family members, which contribute to the family members' survival and well-being. Families' unique histories, traditions, beliefs, and cultures are valuable resources that children bring with them to school and use to create meaning of their world (Gadsden 1998, 1999).

This type of knowledge is often referred to as *multiple literacies*. Multiple literacies encompass a variety of ways of reading text and reading the world (Dantas and Manyak 2010). Traditionally, school-based academic writing programs do not take into account the rich cultural experiences that individuals bring to the table (Compton-Lilly 2004; Moll et al. 1992). The fact that students' "funds of knowledge" are not often tapped into in the classroom results in a disconnect between home and school life (Taylor 1997). The suggested activities in this book capitalize on these "funds," thus bridging the gap between home and school culture.

While past experience shapes and molds who individuals are and how they make sense of their world, how they explain and articulate these experiences also aids in constructing meaning (Bruner 1990). According to Dyson and Genishi (1994, 2), "we all have a basic need for story," which they define as an organization of "experiences into tales of important happenings." Denman (1991, 4) states that stories are "lenses through which we view and review all of human experiences." Narratives allow individuals to use storytelling as a vehicle for understanding within certain social contexts (Young 2000).

Rock Star Tip

Reading and writing are social activities. Students should engage daily with others, drawing inspiration and bringing personal experiences to all literacy activities.

Individuals lead "storied lives" (Connelly and Clandinin 1990, 2), and narratives are part of the rich literacies that individuals possess yet are often devalued in the academic setting and within academic culture. Knowing that the world, from a narrative point of view, is full of stories based on past experiences and prior knowledge, educators should reflect these ideas in both theory and practice (Hollie, 2012). Because the role of narrative in meaning making is important, education at all levels should allow individuals to use the literacies they possess to enhance and deepen the learning experience they take part in at school and at home. In addition to using "funds of knowledge" to help build a bridge between home and school when designing curriculum and professional development, it is important that educators and researchers recognize the impact life histories have on instruction. For education to be relevant and effectively reach students of all ages, educators are encouraged to embrace the role the past plays on the present and how these events are explained through the use of engagements that allow students to convey and communicate these stories.

As you read the *Writing to Think*, section on page 23, notice how the activities capitalize on the tenets and principles outlined above. Writing Breaks (page 30) allow students to process and reflect on their content while making connections with their own lives. Writing Breaks allow for fast, short responses to the material, allowing students to make personal connections and insights. Some of the strategies in the following sections, such as Heard, Refute, and Question (page 91), Social Media Summaries (page 81), and Alpha-Boxes (page 63), allow students to activate prior knowledge and make connections between what they already know and what they are learning.

Students at the Center

Framing writing from a student-centered perspective is especially important. Because this perspective emphasizes the role of the learner in his or her own learning, classrooms and lessons that use this principle differ from traditional approaches in which the teacher is often the center of instruction. Unlike teacher-centered classrooms, where students are viewed as passive recipients in their knowledge acquisition, the student-centered approach shifts the teacher's role from expert to facilitator. The teacher helps prompt and guide students as they develop and monitor their own learning and understanding. This is rooted in the constructivist theory that, while it is important to recognize the knowledge individuals possess and offer opportunities for students to share and build upon this knowledge, individuals must see themselves as active participants in their learning. According to Dewey (1916), in order for meaningful learning to occur, the individual must be seen as a "sharer or partner" in the activity in order to see himself or herself as part of the activity's success or failure.

Teaching reading and writing from a student-centered perspective allows students to create their own meaning from the content, giving them opportunities to explore their understanding through dialogue and conversation so that the written product is an authentic student-created artifact. Implementing these principles in the classroom means allowing students to take part in assignments that aid them in constructing an understanding of the content while using writing as a tool.

Students are encouraged to use strategies and methods that not only capitalize on their knowledge and interests but allow them to develop and conceptualize their own understanding of a concept or an idea. These are especially beneficial in content-area classrooms where the material and concepts can be dense and difficult to understand.

Embracing the Process

Flower and Hayes's (1981) cognitive process model of writing describes writing as a thinking process of planning, drafting, and revising that is conditioned and shaped by both the writer and the task at hand. These processes or steps are recursive in nature; thus, at any given point, a writer may move from one process to another, revisiting parts of a draft, abandoning a particular topic, or writing in order to pursue other topics. From this standpoint, the act of writing is not linear but dynamic and changing. Each guiding force in writing topic, such as audience and purpose, guides the writing process in different ways. A writer's choices at a given moment affect future writing decisions. From this perspective, less attention is paid to the product created and more to the process of writing.

Much of the writing that occurs in the content-area classroom attends to this somewhat messy process model. As students develop an understanding of topics or ideas, they revise, plan, and think as they go. In most instances, the focus for content writing is not necessarily on the product that is created but on the process that students use when writing to reinforce the content.

Much of the writing that takes place in classrooms never leaves the prewriting or drafting stage. Very few pieces go through the entire process, and even fewer make it to this stage in the content classroom.

How Does Content-Area Writing Look?

So, how does content-area writing look? Untidy. Unfinished. Drafty. And that's how it's supposed to look. Take a look at this text mapping done in a social studies classroom. This is not what anyone would consider a "publishable piece." In most instances, students are never going to get past the initial brainstorming or drafting phase of the writing for the simple fact that there is no real need to do so.

☆ Content-area writing does not have to be confined to notebook paper!

This is not an ELA class where teachers *want* and *need* to see final products that have been through all stages of writing, where revision is just as important as drafting, and publishing is equally as important as brainstorming. Content-area teachers may not want to focus on such things. Instead, they need strategies to make their teaching more effective and meaningful. This is why much of the writing you see in content classrooms looks different from that in ELA classrooms. If teachers try to use the same methods and strategies for writing that are used in ELA classrooms in science, math, or social studies, in many cases, they simply would not work.

The reading and writing done in a social studies class is significantly different from that done in an ELA classroom. The photo below shows a student organizing notes after a social studies lesson. The student's notes and summarizations are short and to the point. This probably will be the student's first and only draft.

☆ Content-area writing does not have to be confined to a desk!

What is useful in social studies classrooms in regard to reading and writing assignments can be vastly different from what is needed in science. Consider the following image from a student's science logbook. Here, writing was used to make observations and notations throughout the experimental process. Aside from the experiment, this may be the only writing collected during this science lesson.

☆ This is an example of a Writing Break conducted in a science classroom. This strategy can be found on pages 30–32.

> - less than one=reduction
> • after measuring the space between the center of dilation and the original figure, multiply the length by the scale factor. Then go that distance after multiplying & intersect through each point

You see, treating reading and writing in content classrooms in the same manner as ELA classrooms is not ideal. In the book *What Content-Area Teachers Should Know about Adolescent Literacy*, the National Institute for Literacy states, "Because writing style and purpose vary across different academic disciplines, content-area teachers must be able to teach students how to write using the text structures and stylistic conventions that are prevalent in their disciplines" (2010, 2).

Think of students who attempt to approach their textbook in the same manner in which they would read a fiction novel. If they are looking for a plot, characters, setting, or a problem, they might be sorely disappointed.

Some students are not sure how to approach different types of texts or even if they should approach them in different ways based on their uniqueness in structure and format. This skill must be taught. When students have to write in the content-area classroom, they often revert to the one type of writing they are most comfortable with. Often, this is narrative. Unfortunately, a story about solving a math problem is not going to score well on the rubric for written mathematical reasoning.

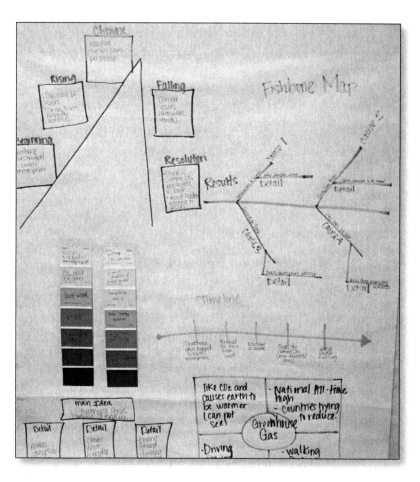

☆ Using a graphic organizer is a meaningful way to incorporate writing into the content-area classroom.

Take a deeper look at the image above. I typically have university students complete this activity in my content-literacy courses. Each group of students is given a different type of article to read. After reading, they circulate through four or five stations to do different types of reading or writing strategies with their articles. Once they are done, they end up with articles that have been dissected using a variety of quick content-literacy strategies. The purpose of this activity is to get students to see that not every strategy works well with every article. For example, models or vocabulary frames work best with articles that have an abundance of content, and time lines work best with articles that have sequential events. However, in this case, I want to highlight that like reading, writing is also multidimensional and should be handled, considered, and integrated differently in content-area classrooms.

Almost all strategies addressed in this book mirror or reflect some of the qualities pictured above. Remember, content-area teachers' goals are very different. Their purpose for incorporating writing may be significantly different from that of an ELA teacher.

How Do I Infuse My Content-Area Lessons with Writing?

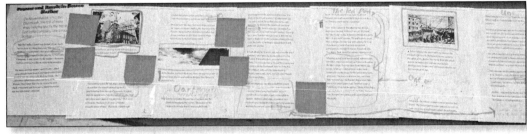

☆ These two articles are from a social studies class. For this activity, students read, rotated, and took notes on an article about the Boston Tea Party.

Working with Your Existing Curriculum

Even with the strictest, most scripted curriculum program, any of the strategies in this book could be incorporated into the content-area classroom with existing textbooks, supplemental materials, or district pacing guides/plans. Plus, they work with any number of standards.

The best way to utilize the strategies in this book with existing curriculum is to identify the standards required in the content area. Use the table of contents as a guide to pinpoint the skills you want students to sharpen, and then modify each activity as needed. (Use the Modification and Content-Area Crossover sections in each activity to get started.)

Time Management

Time seems to be every teacher's greatest challenge, yet incorporating writing into the content-area classroom should not take away from the content curriculum. That is why the writing activities in this book have been selected. They are quick activities that can be implemented in five to ten minutes; they can be used in conjunction with what you are already teaching.

Not sure whether students understand what you just taught? Try a Writing Break (page 30). Unsure of what students know up front about a given concept or subject? Try Heard, Refute, and Question (HRQ) (page 91) or Alpha-Boxes (page 63). Instead of attempting to incorporate a full-blown essay in your class, try having students write Social Media Summaries (page 81). Many of the activities in this book are built on the workshop model; they are living, breathing, working, ongoing assignments that can be short, long, formal, or informal depending on your classroom needs.

Student Engagement

All teachers have had challenging classes. While there is no single quick fix for behavior issues, teachers can reduce—and in some cases, eliminate—some behavior issues by:

- using activities that are of interest (see inventories on pages 105–107)

- allowing for student feedback and discussion

- providing opportunities for students to be mobile; many times, students are bored from sitting still all day—let them move around a bit

- getting to know students so that potential issues can be addressed head-on

- varying the writing assignments implemented in class

The activities in this book can support student engagement. Have students who love social media but can't get interested in classroom content? Use Social Media Summaries (page 81) to interest them in content-area discussions. Have students who enjoy poetry or sports? Utilize the Create a Simile activity (page 49), or complete Sports Summaries (page 71) to encourage participation. Want to illicit more classroom discussions? Conduct Continuum Debate (page 51) or play Red-Light, Green-Light Evidence (page 40). Have students who need movement breaks during the day? Utilize Trailers, Recaps, and Reviews (page 73) to get students moving and interacting with their peers.

Author's Thoughts

Once I conducted professional development at a local school. The principal and assistant principal specifically asked me to visit a fifth grade classroom because the teacher had enormous difficulty with behavior in this class. Before I went to the class, I learned some information about the students. The class consisted of mainly boys, and many of them enjoyed sports. When I arrived for my lesson, I brought the book *The Crossover* by Kwame Alexander. This book is written entirely in prose and follows a middle school basketball player and his twin brother through a particularly tumultuous season.

I intended to read about 20 pages of the book, but 100 pages later (and a promise to come back the next day), I realized that these students, who were labeled as "major behavior problems," had been in the palm of my hand for 45 minutes. Yes, I read to them, but they also wrote with me, answered questions, had good dialogue, and were engaged.

Now, I am not naive enough to believe that they would behave this way for me every day or that in any way their good behavior was a product of my excellent teaching. It was not. Instead, it was a mixture of a small written task, engaging literature, their interest, and room for discussion that made this class perform so well.

Making Content-Area Writing Work for All Learners

Reading and Writing Below Grade Level

One way to address the challenge of capturing the attention of students who struggle with reading and writing is to differentiate reading and writing tasks. While you may use the textbook as a resource, bring in additional text material in a variety of grade levels and formats. Students need to see that some types of writing are structured differently, include different text features, and use specific traits that all combine to create a unique composition.

Recently, while teaching a unit on the dangers of football, it was easy to locate a number of multi-leveled articles that addressed several aspects of the topic. A few of the articles were written in more accessible formats, with numerous pictures and captions. Some were written below grade level, and others were written above grade level, with attention paid to the statistical data regarding football. Because there was such a wide variety of texts available, it was simple to pick and choose those that best fit the needs of each student; students were able to understand the concept and complete the task with ease.

In the content-area classroom, differentiating the text format and complexity may be a way to scaffold content for students who read and write below grade level. There are several educational websites devoted to diverse text across content areas. If you are looking for content-area informational text, try TIME For Kids (timeforkids.com). TIME For Kids specializes in interesting informational texts suitable for all grade levels. Recently, I had a conversation with a media specialist who raved about using the Georgia databases such as Discus (scdiscus.org) and GALILEO (galileo.usg.edu) to locate differentiated reading materials for students. She was thrilled about the plethora of material available for teachers. Using article databases are fast ways to differentiate content.

Another useful source is News ELA (newsela.com). This online repository of news articles covers a variety of interest topics for all content areas. One of the best features of the site is its ability to level the articles based on the reading ability of the student. Instead of assigning the same article to all students, each text can be tailored to the students' reading levels. Some articles also have a second-language feature that translates the article into Spanish. This feature also yields benefits in the foreign-language classroom. Teachers can place the English and Spanish articles side by side for comparisons or have the students read the English article first so that they have a sense of what the text is about. This may make comprehension easier when they begin reading the Spanish article, since they will have prior knowledge about the main idea and details of the article. Conversely, reading an article in Spanish may prepare ELLs to better comprehend English articles.

Modify the Activity

Many teachers have students who are faced with challenges that are not always academic. Nonacademic problems, such as lack of organizational skills, can have major academic impacts in the classroom. One way teachers can combat some academic and nonacademic challenges is to modify each activity, either in product or process. Thoughtful modifications can significantly impact student engagement and performance in the content-area classroom. Each activity in this book has a modification and an extension section for this purpose.

Meeting students where they are is something that can help them get to the final product. Students can feel overwhelmed with vocabulary they do not understand, passages they can't read independently, written language that is highly sophisticated, and tasks that include multi-step

© *Shell Education*

complex pieces. I propose meeting students where they are first and then working to get them to the ultimate goal. Some ways of doing this are to break down the activity into smaller parts, give students ownership of the task, and gauge their interest levels.

Break It Down

Sometimes, the way we approach a task or skill should be modified. For example, a large task can be broken down into small sections. By doing so, students are able to complete the final product by finishing all the smaller pieces that together make up the culminating assignment. Consider grading each section independently of the final product. Students who struggle with completing the entire project may find it easier to handle one small part of it at a time. This way, they can receive grades for the smaller tasks completed along the way. This modification, even without grading each component, will lend itself to more organized final projects. Students who struggle with tasks with multiple components or varied information that needs to be synthesized or who are working in groups will be able to plan their time and attack writing assignments in smaller chunks instead of a large, daunting one.

Giving Students Ownership

Students work better when they have a vested interest in the process and the product. This is why, whenever possible, students should be included in the design and development of projects, readings, assignments, and/or final presentations. This can be difficult when a curriculum is mandated or reading lists are nonnegotiable. However, allowing students' input (where applicable) can be as simple as having them assist in generating topics for writing and can yield positive academic results.

For example, when teaching persuasive writing, it is best to allow students to generate their own ideas for topics. This works well because their ideas are often centered on current issues in their schools or lives. Get students involved as much as possible. Bring in supplemental materials that will spark interest. In order to increase motivation in students, I would suggest these quick tips:

★ Develop activities that capitalize on student interest.

★ Allow student input into assignments when possible.

★ Get to know your students as people first, and students second. (Use interest inventories on pages 105–107 to start this process.)

Use Interest Inventories

While the easiest way to gauge students' interests in the content-area classroom is to have conversations with them, another way is to use interest inventories. Interest inventories are simple questionnaires that allow students to list items they like, such as television and movies they enjoy or favorite pastimes. This activity is quick and gives students opportunities to share things about themselves with you in a low-stakes manner.

Interest inventories can be used to get to know your students and what they enjoy, but they can also be used to gain insight into how students perceive an entire content area, selected topics, or components of a subject. Plus, they may help you incorporate activities and reading materials that reflect student interest.

I typically issue interest inventories at the beginning of the quarter, semester, or year (see pages 105–107 for samples). Once I collect them, even a cursory glance provides me with information about which classes had high concentrations of sports fanatics, which enjoyed post-apocalyptic television and movies, and which had younger siblings.

This strategy was especially helpful in my classroom because of the large number of students I taught. It helped me modify and differentiate writing assignments by class, by group, and in some cases, by student. For example, while informational writing might be my focus for all classes, the materials and supplements I used varied for each class period. Although I chose to use one main supplemental text for all classes, the additional texts and examples varied based on each class.

Author's Thoughts

When I think about myself as a literate person and consider all the aspects of it, I think of all the types of literacy skills, strategies, and competencies that collectively shaped me as an individual. Like a passport, I have literacy "stamps" of places, competencies, and literacies that I possess and use. No one component is more important than another. Instead, these pieces fit together like a puzzle. Each piece is unique, has its own attributes and values, and contributes to the overall conceptualization of my literate self in a different way. Plus, like a passport that shows the locations that travelers visit frequently, my literacy passport includes some skills or strategies with multiple stamps.

What do I mean by this? What does traveling to the same destination over and over offer? Familiarity? Deeper knowledge of an area? Closer contact with local residents? Correspondingly, what does this mean for a traveler who has only been to a destination once? Which location would the traveler feel most comfortable discussing or taking a companion to? The same is true for literacy. I may be well versed in narrative writing; I know how to employ a variety of techniques and devices to better convey the overall message of the story. However, the same may not necessarily be true when it comes to constructing an argument. Yes, I may know how to do it, but I may not have extensive knowledge or experience in crafting an argument in several disciplines.

Here is where the water gets muddy: if you think about your students and all the tasks, skills, and demands that they encounter on a daily basis, they are faced with mounting challenges of navigating between disciplines and texts, with the ultimate goal being comprehension and understanding. For a novice reader and writer, this can be difficult. That is why writing in every discipline on a daily basis is an absolute necessity in order for students to be successful not only in their academic careers but in their daily lives.

Writing to Think

When you think about the writing you do on a daily basis, fully polished formal compositions are probably rare. Most writing will stay in an unpolished, rough form. How often do you write a final draft of your grocery list? How about your to-do list? Now, think about that email you are sending to your boss—is that more polished than your grocery list? Why? The audience, purpose, and mode are different. However, if you were to compare the number of writings you complete that actually become more refined, they would probably be dwarfed by those that stay rough in nature. In many cases, our rough drafts are our only drafts—they never make it through to the final publishing stage. We live our lives through a series of rough drafts. These are the types of writings that are most helpful on a daily basis since they help us to organize thoughts, synthesize information, and make sense of the world around us.

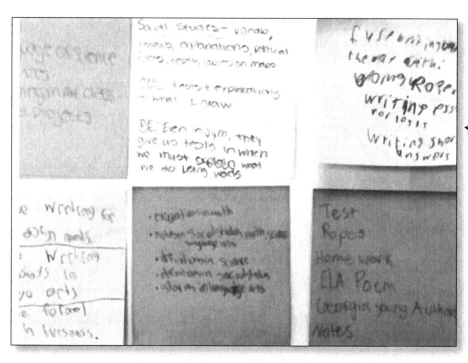

☆ Sticky notes serve as an effective vehicle to jot down thinking in the content-area classroom.

Writing can be a valuable strategy to use in your classroom for thinking and processing information. Writing in this form can help students process material, work through the difficult parts of a new concept, engage in the subject matter (Daniels, Zemelman, and Steineke 2007), and develop a deeper understanding for a skill or composition (Langer and Applebee 1987). In many instances, the types of thinking that occur on paper are evolutionary in nature. In other words, at the beginning of the task, students probably have not conceptualized the entire nature of the piece. Instead, they are working through their thoughts on paper.

The notion that writing is a tool for thinking allows writing to become a vehicle for exploration and discovery. It opens windows into students' thought processes, the writing decisions made when drafting, and the thinking that occurs when one makes decisions about just what and how to write. Instead of viewing writing as a linear process with a starting and stopping point, writing is more of a recursive process, one in which writers are making decisions, shifting back and forth from different parts of the process, and revising as they go. During this time, opportunities for exploration of topics, elaboration of ideas, and revision of thoughts can occur.

Using writing as a tool for thinking attends to these major principles:

★ Much of this writing is unpolished and unfinished.

★ A variety of writing strategies should be implemented in an effort to make sure students do not get blocked by a particular strategy.

★ This writing should not be evaluated in the same manner in which other more formal writings are evaluated.

★ This writing is meant to address content understanding and not to refine composition skills or improve grammar or spelling performance.

Drumming for More

Want to know more about the cognitive processes involved in writing? Check out Flower and Hayes's seminal text on the subject, "A Cognitive Process Theory of Writing" (1981, 366). Here are the four key points on which their research is based:

1. The process of writing is a set of distinctive thinking processes that writers orchestrate or organize during the act of composing.

2. These processes have a hierarchical, highly embedded organization in which any given process can be embedded within any other.

3. The act of composing is a goal-directed thinking process, guided by the writer's own growing network of goals.

4. Writers create their own goals in two key ways: by generating goals and sub-goals that embody the writer's developing sense of purpose, and then, at times, by changing goals or establishing new ones based on what has been learned in the act of writing.

Who's the Writing For?

Two vital elements for teachers to consider when using writing as a tool for thinking are *audience* and *purpose*. Some student writing is done for others, and some is done simply for the student. While I believe most genres can transcend this distinction, it is important for students to value themselves as primary audiences for some writing and to think of metacognition as a purpose for writing. In some cases, this works best when students have had some time away from the piece so they can look at the entries with fresh eyes.

Rock Star Tip

While writing-to-learn activities should not be graded in the same manner as other writing activities, they have to be read and used by someone besides the creator. Students should be held accountable for the activity as a vehicle for learning.

Written Conversations (page 27) and Writing Breaks (page 30) are primarily writing activities completed for the student. Regardless of the audience or format for the writing, the important component is that the writing allows students to think through the content and material, thus assisting them in comprehending the overall point of the content.

Writing-to-Think Strategies

When writing is used as a tool for thinking, that tool can be as varied as the thoughts of the individual. To be successful, teachers should consider the ways in which their students think. Students need time to think about what they've learned, reflecting on their understanding, and how the new learning connects to past and future learning.

There are a number of activities that can be used to promote writing as a tool for thinking. However, the strategies included in this section are specific to guiding students to process content material, reflect on their thinking, and make sense of the material they learn in their content-area classrooms.

You will notice that many of the strategies in this section center on dialogue, conversation, and discussions. Oral conversations are powerful vehicles for understanding in the classroom and the world around you. Probst's (1988) suggests that classrooms allow students time to engage in and interact with texts (and content) through discussions that are shaped by the students' goals.

Written Conversations build on classroom discussions in which students communicate ideas and give students time to "talk through" material on paper. These activities allow students opportunities to practice their writing skills as a means of communication. Written Conversations are exactly what they sound like—conversations on paper. These activities are quick, can be implemented at a moment's notice, and serve as a vehicle for understanding.

The intent of the remainder of this section is to give content-area teachers a group of strategies that they can use as tools for thinking in the classroom:

★ Written Conversations 27

★ Writing Breaks 30

★ Dialogue Journals 33

Author's Thoughts

☆ After a full content lesson, students write their ideas on note cards and post them on the board during a class discussion.

In one of my university courses, I gave an informal assignment for an upcoming class. I wanted my students to think about their writing process, pay attention to how they revise as they go, think through the construction of the writing, and make decisions about what will be included based on the format and audience. I explained what I wanted them to do, and each one of them made notations in their notebooks about the assignment. Following my explanation, I had each student read back the notes he or she had written. While I expected that there would be some subtle differences in each based on individual word choice or voice, some descriptions were drastically different. Each one captured what I had asked for but in dramatically different ways.

As we discussed how this happened, students remarked that they had written in formats that would help them understand the assignment later, included information that allowed them to make connections, and were thinking through the parameters of the assignment as they wrote. With this simple example, we discussed how writing is unique to each individual. We also talked about how teachers often provide instructions or material to the entire class, only to have students misunderstand or misinterpret what was heard. During that class period, each student, all practicing teachers, heard the exact same words, yet each wrote their own interpretation. Why? Each student is unique. Each student attended to different parts of my instructions based on the importance they assigned them.

Written Conversations

Background

Dialogue is one way we make sense of the world. How often have you had a problem, called a friend to ask for advice, and then spent the whole time talking about the problem instead of listening to the advice? Did you feel better after the conversation? Probably. Why? Because talking through issues and confusions helps cement understanding.

Written Conversations can be used for this purpose during a content-area lesson. The back-and-forth nature allows teachers to assess what students are understanding, what misconceptions they may have, or what questions they still have on in any given topic.

Benefits

- This activity requires students to work on effective written communication skills; they only respond in writing.

- This form of writing is familiar to students and does not require frontloading or explicit teaching.

- Spelling, grammar, and abbreviated texts are acceptable for this activity. Students should write clearly so their peers are able to read, understand, and follow the written conversation.

Procedure

1. Provide a specific question or prompt to students.

2. Give them one to two minutes to write their responses.

3. Then, have students pass their responses to their classmates.

4. Have partners craft a written response to their peers for another one to two minutes. **Note:** There should be little to no talking while students write their thoughts and respond to their peers.

Modifications

- Instead of giving students a prompt, have students write questions or comments about the lesson for their classmates.

- Have a snowball fight. Have students put their names on their papers, crumple them up, and toss them across the room. Students grab paper snowballs, open them, respond to their classmates, crumple them up, and throw the notes back. (Repeat as many times as necessary.)

- Try a text message conversation. This informal writing allows students to capitalize on their text message knowledge. Plus, students get to use abbreviations, acronyms, and emoticons that they typically use when texting.

- If you would prefer a more formal assignment, have a written conversation between you and your students. **Note:** In order to manage the volume of messages, make and display a response or schedule so students know when they should expect a response.

 Drumming for More

Try using Today's Meet (todaysmeet.com) for a digital take on this activity.

Extensions

- Extend this activity with digital conversations. Use websites like Today's Meet to set up virtual rooms for classroom chats. Moderate the discussions, and close chats once students are done.

- Worried that some students may have difficulty finding partners to respond to their written conversation? Worried that some may *only* pair with their friends? Try alternating between allowing students to choose their writing partners and using predetermined teacher-made pairs.

Content-Area Crossover

- Social Studies—This is an activity that requires analytical skills and synthesizing of multiple materials and perspectives. Students can use Written Conversations to reflect on classroom lessons, state opinions and oppositions, or pose additional questions to you or classmates about social studies topics.

- Math—Written Conversations could be a useful tool to enhance students' abilities to show mathematical thinking when solving problems. Written communication forces students to break down their thought process into small, digestible pieces, explaining step by step to you or their peers how they arrived at their answers.

Author's Thoughts

When I was a little girl, my grandmother worked second shift at a battery plant. During this time, her youngest daughter, my Aunt Stacy, lived at home with her, since Stacy was still in school. Because of their disjointed schedules, they rarely saw each other during the weekdays. I remember as a young child going to their house and seeing conversations between my grandmother and aunt written on notebook paper—and in some cases, napkins when there was no paper. My mother and I would sit at the table, read the notes and responses, and catch up on the week's events at home without ever speaking to either of them.

These written conversations were a part of my family's daily life and served in place of oral conversations. These written conversations were the dialogue between my grandmother and aunt, which fulfilled a communicative purpose that time and proximity could not. By using them as a vehicle for delivery, they were still able to communicate, converse, and respond on a daily basis.

Written Conversations (cont.)

- Science—To incorporate Written Conversations into the science classroom, pose a specific question to the class. For example, for a biome lesson, you could ask, *What types of animals live in the tundra?* or *What types of plants grow in the desert?* If you have students in your class who like science fiction, pose scenario questions instead. Some sample scenarios are: *What would you do if Earth ran out of water?* and *What are some ways we could create/ make/source water?*

- Art—Written Conversations can be used to create poetry or songs. Introduce a topic, and have students compose a collaborative poem or song. Have students contribute one line to the final product and present it to the class.

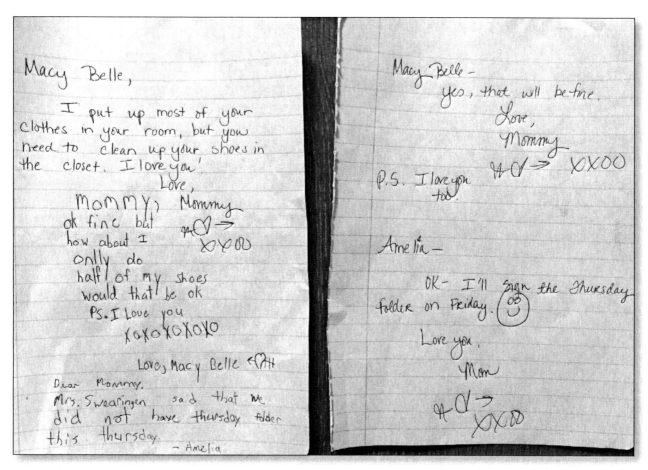

☆ This is an example of Written Conversations in my family. This activity is an organized way to document students' thinking, especially for the content teachers who teach multiple classes and see over 50 students in one given school day.

Writing Breaks

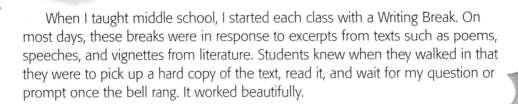

Author's Thoughts

When I taught middle school, I started each class with a Writing Break. On most days, these breaks were in response to excerpts from texts such as poems, speeches, and vignettes from literature. Students knew when they walked in that they were to pick up a hard copy of the text, read it, and wait for my question or prompt once the bell rang. It worked beautifully.

Background

When students need to learn a lot of content in a short time, Writing Breaks can be effective. Stopping to write periodically gives students an opportunity to gather their thoughts. Anything in the lesson content, class discussions, or students' general interests can spark an idea for a Writing Break.

Benefits

- Writing Breaks are short bursts of writing.

- Teachers can use them at prime times when content is dense and difficult to process or when you are at a transition or stopping point.

Rock Star Tip

Prompt ideas:

- What does this text/image/video remind you of?

- Make a list of words that describe this text/image/video.

- How does this text/image/video relate to what we talked about yesterday?

- Make a list of all the topic's concepts you find in this text/image/video.

- This activity is informal, and students should focus more on content than writing mechanics.

Procedure

1. Teach a subject-specific concept or several concepts that require students to synthesize.

2. Announce the "break" to the class.

3. Have students write for three to five minutes, in any format, about the material. Have students focus only on their learning and not on grammar, spelling, and penmanship.

Modifications

- Give students a focused objective (word count, sentence allotment, inclusion of focus words, etc.) when completing their Writing Break.

- Complete a "text break" instead. Have students stop to write as if they were sending a text to a friend. Allow students to use shorthand, abbreviations, symbols, and emoticons to represent words and phrases as they would when texting.

Extensions

- If time permits, and as needed, allow students to discuss their writing as a class, with groups, or partners.

- Give students time to review previous Writing Breaks to gather evidence of their growth during a unit.

- Guide students to highlight or mark important ideas in their writing.

- Have students revisit their writing later in the unit to correct any misconceptions they had before they learned more about the concept.

- Have students swap writing with partners and elaborate on or discuss writing.

- Have students collect their writing pieces over the course of a unit of study to create an informal portfolio of their thinking about the unit or a big idea.

Content-Area Crossover

- Social Studies—Writing Breaks in social studies could be geared toward explaining, applying, or questioning what students have learned. When starting a new topic, have students write everything they know about the topic before introducing it. Or, have students draw parallels between historical and current events.

- Science—Use a Writing Break as an opportunity for students to dig deeper into a science topic. In second grade, students study plants and how they grow. Apply this to what keeps humans growing, or what might happen if certain plants stopped growing. Writing Breaks can be used in the science classroom to pose science fiction "what if" scenarios because it encourages critical thinking and gives students opportunities to draw on what they know to prove or disprove their reasoning. Also, the science fiction approach seems to be pretty high interest in upper-elementary and middle grades.

- Math—The focus of a Writing Break may be calculations based or strategy based in the math content classroom.

- Art—When studying an artist, a period of work, or movement, have students use Writing Breaks to digest, sketch, or reflect on the new material. Question students about an artist's motive or reason for creating a specific work.

- Other—Writing Breaks are effective for nonacademic matters and sensitive issues such as bullying and discrimination and can be used when students need to stop to reflect on their actions.

Rock Star Tip

Ever have an impromptu moment when you need to pause your instruction for a few minutes? A Writing Break can be a useful 'Plan B' when these moments arise! Look for signs of confusion, questioning, and inattention during long spans of instruction. That may be your signal to introduce a Writing Break activity into your lesson.

Writing Breaks *(cont.)*

SKMBT_ ✕ | 📄 Lankshe ✕ | 📊 Teens, S ✕ | 🅱 Writing ✕ | 🍎 iCloud I ✕ | Ⓐ A-Z Ind ✕ | Schedul ✕

rharper7/Downloads/SKMBT_55216022916572.pdf

Everything I know about 3D shapes:

- They can be cut to form cross sections
- Their volume can be found which is how much that 3D shape can hold
- Their surface area can be found which is the area of all the faces together
- 3D shapes can be turned into nets which basically just unfold them
- 3D shapes can have any number of faces
- 3D shapes can also have any number of edges
- 3D shapes have a length, width, and height
- Can be sliced to form 2D figures
- cubes are rectangular prisms both are
- 3D shapes can be found in real life not only in the text book
- When finding the volume of a 3D shape your answer is always cubic units
- when finding surface area of a 3D shape your answer is always squared units
- Sometimes 3D shapes have vertices) and/or vertexes)

☆ This Writing Break sample is from a math task titled, "Everything I Know about 3-D Shapes."

51560—Content-Area Writing That Rocks (and Works!) © Shell Education

Dialogue Journals

Background

Dialogue Journals are tools that capitalize on the importance of dialogue and conversation. The journals are kept between a pair of writers (or shared between you and a student). Dialogue Journals offer opportunities for students to respond to content material that they are learning while also conversing on paper with teachers or classmates.

While similar to Written Conversations, Dialogue Journals differ in that, in most cases, students complete entries about given topics, questions, prompts, or ideas. Similarly, students may be required to end their entry with questions for their partners, depending on the scope and nature of the assignment.

Benefits

- Dialogue Journal responses are structured.

- Dialogue Journals are effective tools for thinking and allowing partners to build on ideas and understandings.

- This activity is informal; students' main objective is to convey ideas.

Procedure

1. Present a question or thought to students.

2. Give students time to write a journal response addressing the prompt.

3. Collect the journal entries. (**Note:** If your objective is to get an immediate glimpse of what students are thinking, stop here and provide a teacher response. If you are using this activity in a larger unit, allow students to keep ongoing journals until the end of the unit.)

4. Ask students to respond to their partners' entries. **Note:** This can be done in class or at home.

Modification

- Instead of a full Dialogue Journal, have students complete dialogue postcards. This writing is much shorter and requires students to summarize their ideas in one paragraph.

Extensions

- Have students take key entries from their journals that were especially interesting, powerful, or thought provoking and write note-card-length extensions of their entries. This allows students to extend the assignment but still keep it fairly brief, which can appeal to reluctant writers.

Content-Area Crossover

- Social Studies—Have students create Dialogue Journals to correspond with a historical figure or pose questions from the perspective of different stakeholders of a historical event. Have students write to someone in the future explaining what life is like now.

- Math—Pose a variety of questions about the same math task. For example, you may ask students to describe the processes they used to solve a math problem. Later in the week, ask students to explain the vocabulary used in the same task.

- Science—Prompt students to make connections between real-world events and science concepts. Have students write Dialogue Journals to or about a scientist. Have them write to someone in the future explaining what life is like today.

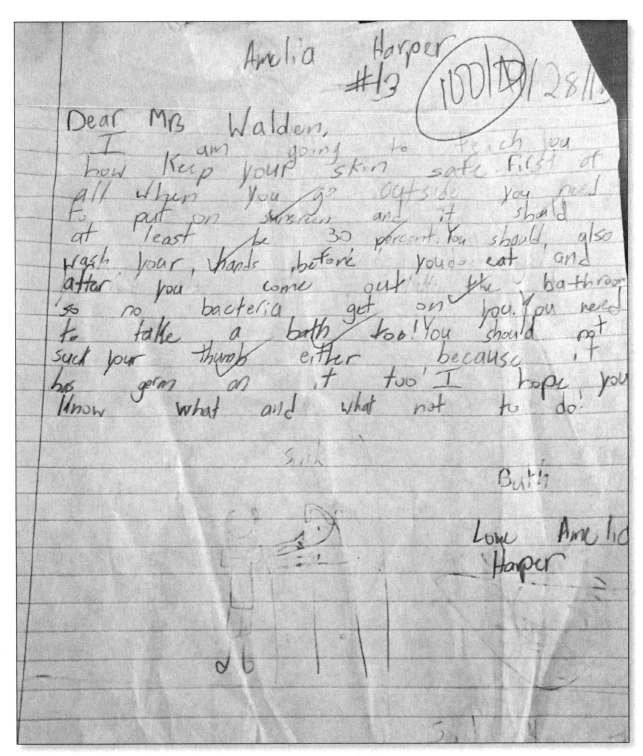

☆ This is a Dialogue Journal entry from a student in a science classroom.

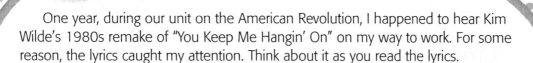

Author's Thoughts

One year, during our unit on the American Revolution, I happened to hear Kim Wilde's 1980s remake of "You Keep Me Hangin' On" on my way to work. For some reason, the lyrics caught my attention. Think about it as you read the lyrics.

"You Keep Me Hangin' On"
(Originally by The Supremes)
Set me free why don't cha babe
Get out of my life, why don't cha, babe
'Cause you don't really love me
You just keep me hangin' on

Set me free, why don't cha, babe
Weren't the American colonists saying this to England?
Get out of my life, why don't cha, babe
You don't really need me
But you keep me hangin' on

Why do you keep a comin' around?
Playing with my heart
Why don't cha get out of my life
And let me make a brand-new start
Didn't the colonists want to start over? Develop a new government?
Let me get over you
The way you've gotten over me, yeah

I used this song as a writing activity for my class that day. I posted the lyrics and asked students to think about the American Revolution and the colonists' problems with England. After some nudging and thinking, students were able to tie historical facts to sections in the lyrics that illustrated those facts. Then, I challenged students to find another song with lyrics that could be related to or tied to our studies of the American Revolution. Yes, it was unorthodox and a little wacky, but it got my students doing something many of them resisted: thinking critically and writing!

Writing to Prove

What exactly is writing to prove? Often, teachers give students writing tasks that require them to explain or prove their answers. Many times, students write to explain something to the reader; on other occasions, they are trying to *prove* to the reader that they know something or can *prove* something through the use of evidence.

Finding evidence is something that must be mastered in all content areas. In some cases, students may struggle with locating quality evidence that adequately justifies their answer. Quite often, they think that their opinions suffice as evidence. Other times, students are able to find and state textual evidence without thinking critically about the proof. Finding textual evidence will not always help students when proving their points in the content-area classroom. In the content-area classroom, students may need to synthesize this skill with content-specific skills, pull information from multiple resources, or couple the two with observations.

Writing to prove requires students to do more than simply state their opinions, answer the questions, or point to the text as a qualifier. Instead, these activities focus on textual evidence, personal/human experiences, analytical skills, and observations as a means of proving a point. For some students, this may be challenging because they believe that their opinions or one example is enough. It isn't.

Writing to prove is important for a number of reasons:

★ The ability to use evidence to prove a claim can assist students in articulating an argument.

★ A number of high-stakes assessments have started incorporating "command of evidence" questions, which require students to write, support, and prove.

★ Finding and using evidence to support claims assists students in practicing their synthesizing and analytical writing skills.

In this section, you will find several activities that can be used as tools for proving and finding evidence in the content-area class. Each can be tailored to fit your objectives and classroom needs. The following strategies can be used as tools for proving.

★ Paint-Strip Evidence 38

★ Red-Light, Green-Light Evidence 40

★ Textual Evidence Throw Down 42

★ Picture This! 45

★ Do This, Not That Recipe 47

★ Create a Simile 49

★ Continuum Debate 51

★ iPod List 53

Paint-Strip Evidence

Background

Paint strips are useful tools for writing and organizing evidence. Because the strips are already divided into parts, you can designate each section for a specific type of evidence or descriptor. For example, if this strategy is being used with one resource, you may elect to give specific categories for each of the seven sections on the paint strip. Alternatively, students may use multiple resources to locate evidence about a particular figure's contributions to a historical event and house this information on one paint strip. Paint strips are great tools for students to use for listing evidence on any subject.

Benefits

- This activity will appeal to the reluctant writer.

- This activity requires little writing; students can write in fragments, phrases, or snippets of words.

- This activity forces students to be succinct. Students need to give specific, not general, examples to support their claims.

- This activity can be modified to include quotations, reinforcing how to reference a source.

- This activity can be used periodically during longer units or serve as an informal assessment during one lesson.

Procedure

1. Provide a specific task or question to students. Students should know exactly what type of evidence to look for.

2. Provide students with the sources or materials from which they are locating evidence. **Note:** If students are using multiple sources, explain how they should list citations on the paint strip.

3. Hand out paint strips (see page 115), and give students time to study material and gather evidence.

Modifications

- Differentiate this assignment by cutting the strips based on how many pieces of evidence you want students to locate.

- Have students combine text evidence with personal evidence. Assign one section on the paint strip for personal evidence and another for textual evidence. This allows students to dig deeper, offer personal examples, and use content-area materials when writing to prove.

Extensions

- Students use the evidence listed on the paint strip to construct fully developed sentences about the material covered.

- Use the paint strips in a larger unit. Have students return to their paint strips to assess whether their evidence held up, needs to be modified, or is still relevant.

Content-Area Crossover

- Social Studies—Have students find evidence about a particular historical figure, key features of a geographic area, descriptions of a particular battle or war strategy, or major components/features of a specific time period.

- Math—Have students list justifications and evidence for their chosen method for solving a problem, draw diagrams and figures as evidence for a problem, or list math vocabulary and meanings that can be used as evidence.

51560—Content-Area Writing That Rocks (and Works!) © Shell Education

- Science—Have students record observations and data for an experiment. For example, students can list key features of an organism as evidence for its subsequent classification, list evidence supporting or opposing a particular position in science, such as genetic engineering, or list evidence for how something occurs or is created by nature (coral reefs) compared to something man-made (piers or jetties).

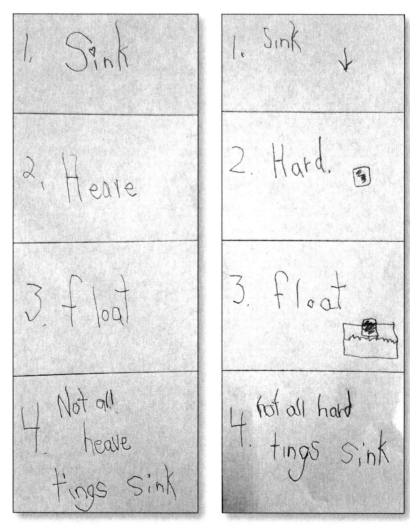

☆ This Paint-Strip Evidence activity was conducted in a second grade science class. Students were conducting experiments to test their sink/float theory. Students needed to use evidence to write their conclusions.

Red-Light, Green-Light Evidence

Background

Sometimes students have difficulty determining what types of evidence are considered credible. With the Red-Light, Green-Light activity, students locate evidence, record it on sticky notes, and then classify it on chart paper based on the quality of the evidence.

This activity can be used after the Paint-Strip Evidence activity on page 38 as a way of extending and returning to students' initial ideas. Use the graphic organizer on page 112 as an individual student handout to record writing for this activity.

Benefits

- This activity involves a lot of movement; students will move around the classroom to complete this activity.

- This assignment is informal. Students are encouraged to write in their most informational and comfortable formats. Writing needs to be clear enough for their peers to read.

- This activity is quick. Allow three to five minutes for each portion of the activity.

- This activity is low stakes. Since students are not required to list their names, there is less pressure to get the right answer.

Procedure

1. Display a Red-Light, Green-Light Evidence template in the classroom (see page 112).

2. Have students record evidence on the topic being studied on sticky notes and place them on the floor.

3. Have students circulate the room and pick up random pieces of evidence from the floor.

4. Have students read the evidence chosen and place it on the appropriate chart paper. **Note:** Red-Light Evidence examples are those that are not on topic, are weak and loosely defined, or include extraneous details that do not serve as quality pieces of evidence. Green-Light Evidence examples are those that include relevant information; have strong, well-thought-out reasoning; and are directly tied to the phenomena in need of evidence. Yellow-Light examples include evidence that students are unsure of.

Modifications

- Use the Yellow-Light section of the chart for unknown information or for ideas that you will revisit, debate, and/or discuss later.

- Worried that you have too many students to warrant this kind of movement in the classroom? Have students circulate in small groups, limiting the number of students out of their seats at one time.

- Create a shared Google Doc™ where students can add and edit their classmates' evidence examples virtually.

- If you teach more than one section of a course, have one class complete the initial-evidence activity as "exit slips." Have the next class pick up the evidence and place them on the correct light as "tickets-in" as they enter the class.

- If you have more than one category that you would like students to find evidence for, use this activity with the Textual-Evidence Throw Down activity on page 42.

Extensions

- Challenge students to rank the evidence by quality and strength. Since this strategy requires students to classify information and evidence, it provides the opportunity for students to critically examine evidence and determine whether it meets the criteria as a strong example of evidence.

- Challenge students to modify or revise Red-Light Evidence to make it fit the standard for Green-Light Evidence

Content-Area Crossover

- Social Studies—Students can use Red-Light, Green-Light Evidence when locating quality evidence on a variety of topics that include information on historical figures or examples of battle strategies.

- Math—The Red-Light, Green-Light Evidence activity guides students to create a quality constructed response or justification for their mathematical decisions. This activity could prove to be helpful as students begin to work on constructing extended responses that require quality evidence and justifications.

- Science—Any classroom that requires students to analyze their thinking would benefit from using this activity. In the science classroom, have students select the best evidence to include in a lab report, observation notes, or evidence of scientific advances that changed the trajectory of the world.

Rock Star Tip

It is important to explain to students that information in the red light does not necessarily mean it is wrong. Instead, it may mean that it is not the *best* evidence for the topic. Frame the activity as a learning experience for all students so that they are not embarrassed and/or ashamed if this happens to their evidence. Sometimes, Red-Light Evidence for a certain concept can become Green-Light Evidence for another.

Textual-Evidence Throw Down

Background

Finding evidence in a text can be intimidating for some students. Part of this could be because many of the text sources used for gathering information are fairly lengthy and include academic vocabulary. Sometimes students may not be sure where the evidence should come from, how it should be written, and how much is enough.

Textual-Evidence Throw Down includes the whole class in this process. Every student needs to find one detail, record it, and then discuss it with the class. Students "throw down" their ideas and interact with their peers to determine if information is valid and strong.

Benefits

- This activity will appeal to the tactile learner.

- This activity requires students to move around the room and engage with their peers.

- Students practice listening and speaking skills during this activity.

Procedure

1. Make a list of the big ideas and/or themes you want students to find evidence for. This may include one idea or several. Label a large sheet of paper for each focus, and place them on the floor of your classroom. (**Note:** This can also be done on the wall and/or board.)

2. Distribute sticky notes for students to record their evidence.

3. Have students circulate and list evidence for each of the categories. Students should place the sticky note in the appropriate pile on the floor.

4. Have students return to their seats and hold a class discussion on some of the evidence in each category.

☆ This is an example of a high school Social Studies classroom where students completed the Textual-Evidence Throw Down activity.

Textual-Evidence Throw Down (cont.)

Modification

- Have students take the evidence from the Textual-Evidence Throw Down and sort them using the Red-Light, Green-Light Evidence activity on pages 40–41 to determine if the evidence is accurate.

Extensions

- If you would like to extend this writing into a longer formal writing piece, have students return to the evidence piles, choose new pieces of evidence (ones they did not write), and construct sentences or responses about the pieces of evidence.

- Instead of students using the evidence to construct a sentence with that information, have them elaborate or expound on the information.

- Students should continue to collect evidence from the piles until they have enough information to draft paragraphs or multi-paragraph compositions about the material.

- Have students take pieces of evidence from the floor and construct potential assessment questions in which the evidence on the sticky note is the answer.

- Allow students to create a cooperative response essay with partners or groups. One student writes a sentence and then passes the paper to another student to write another sentence. After each student finishes a sentence using evidence from the activity, the student passes it to a classmate. Students should go back to the evidence piles and locate another piece of information that works with the essay. This allows partners to work together cooperatively on a written activity, locating pertinent information and evidence to support a longer writing assignment.

Content-Area Crossover

- Social Studies—This activity can be used during history lessons. Have students start by making a claim about a historical event or person and then progress to locating the actual evidence to support their thesis statements.

- Math—Use the Textual-Evidence Throw Down activity to reinforce what constitutes effective evidence when justifying answers to math problems.

- Science—Use this activity to have students compare two topics taught. For example, students can compare the benefits of solar power with the use of fossil fuels. Once students have thrown down the qualities or benefits of each type of power source, they can then choose an example and find evidence from multiple sources to support or refute the claim.

- Art—This activity can be used to determine and justify why a particular painting is an example of a period or a movement.

Rock Star Tip
Make sure students have adequate time to complete the task but not so much that they get off task.

Author's Thoughts

When teaching the Textual-Evidence Throw Down activity, I began by listing the main characters of a novel and placing them on the floor. Then, I had students take sticky notes and circulate the room, throwing down character traits that could be used to describe each character. Once students had compiled enough words for each character, they were instructed to choose a character from the story, choose three character traits from the pile, and use the novel to find textual evidence that supported each trait.

Students had to use the text to cite the evidence on the back of the sticky note. If students found multiple examples of evidence that supported a specific character trait, they would attach another sticky note to the original one. After students found enough evidence, they were given two more sticky notes, which they used to write a topic and a conclusion sentence summarizing the specific character and his or her traits. (This will become a paragraph later.) Since this activity was done in steps, students were able to manage the task easily. In addition, since students were only looking for specific examples of evidence that pertained to certain character traits, they were not as easily overwhelmed by the task.

Here's another thought: What do you do if students throw down incorrect information? This could pose a real problem if another student picks up the information and assumes that it is correct. This potential problem occurred to me when I was using this strategy in a science classroom to describe transparent, translucent, and opaque materials. In order to circumvent this possible issue, I made certain to go over the words suggested for each material, checking for accuracy. However, in the interest of saving time, it wasn't possibe to go through each word. As a result, I modified the assignment. Students were instructed to pick up a descriptor from each pile and take it back to their desks. Once they had done so, they used new sticky notes to do one of two things. First, if the information on the sticky notes they picked up was correct, they each took another sticky note and elaborated on that material. Second, if they picked up something that was incorrect on their new sticky notes, they corrected what their classmates had written.

This worked well because it required students to pay attention to the material they were reading and determine if it was correct. Since they never put their names on their sticky notes, no one could tell who got something incorrect.

Picture This!

Background

While textual evidence is important in many content-area classes, credence needs to also be given to analyzing images and non-text features. The Picture This! activity does just that.

In this activity, students are directed to use non-text features to support claims and synthesize material previously taught. Students can practice paying close attention to details and finding evidence outside the text by looking at the titles, subtitles, headings, subheadings, images, captions, or other text features.

Benefits

- This activity appeals to the visual learner.

- Students are able to practice their analytical thinking.

Procedure

1. Ask students to analyze the material.

2. Pose a particular question or state a claim about the material. **Note:** If you are using this activity as a pre-lesson activity, ask inference-based questions. If you are using this activity post-lesson, ask conclusion-based questions.

3. Then, have students locate and list evidence using visual representation(s) on sticky notes to answer the question or support or refute your claim.

Modifications

- Allow students to work with peers to develop evidence. (Have students use previous notes, additional classroom resources, etc.)

- Language learners may benefit from sentence frames, such as: Based on _____, I know _____ . (See the Rock Star Tip for writing frames and prompts.)

Extensions

- Use the evidence that students located by looking at the text features as a springboard to classroom discussions and debates.

- Compare and contrast the evidence located between pieces of evidence from other students in the class.

Content-Area Crossover

- Social Studies—This strategy can be used in a number of content areas and can serve as an initial introduction to any topic. In social studies, use historical photographs to locate evidence from the time period, movie clips for evidence of references to historical events, maps and topographical images to list evidence of specific regions and/or landforms, and primary sources for evidence of period language and events.

Rock Star Tip

Use the prompts below as a starting point when analyzing non-text features:

- What do you notice about this…?

- What information can be gathered?

- Does this remind you of something?

- Is this image a good representation of…?

- Based on these images, what do you think we will be discussing next?

- How does this image connect to the information we just learned?

- If you had to sort these images, what would determine your categories?

• Math—Introducing students to a new topic through visual means is one way to pique the interest of even the most reluctant students. In math, use diagrams and figures to prove certain mathematic principles, or use concepts or video clips for evidence of math concepts or use of math terms.

• Science—In science, use images of genetic codes or markers for students to locate evidence of a specific characteristic or trait, or use images of elements for students to find evidence of that element's properties.

• Art—In art, use paintings and other art forms, and have students list evidence of a specific style or inspiration. Use songs for students to list evidence of tempo, tone, or key and identify the composer or genre. Show images from certain time periods, and have students respond to why people of that time created artwork that looked that way.

Rock Star Tip

You can even use the Picture This! activity as a culminating formal assessment. Visually represent two images, and ask students which one best represents a strategy, a process, a method, or a concept learned. Extend this into a formal writing piece in which students have to justify their claims and refute the other image.

☆ This Picture This! activity was conducted in a high school Social Studies class. Students were asked to highlight important text features and cross out any features not related to the content.

© *Shell Education*

Do This, Not That Recipe

Author's Thoughts

This idea started with a cricket and a cookbook. I had just finished teaching a unit on informational texts and used an article on harvesting crickets for consumption. (They are high in protein.) The students in the class were particularly interested in the cricket section because of its text features. The article included a nutrition table, an image that was to scale of a cricket, and a brief how-to passage that explained the steps to growing your own crickets.

I came home that evening and pulled out a cookbook. You may be familiar with the books *Eat This, Not That* and *Cook This, Not That* by David Zincsenko and Matt Goulding. As I was reading, I was struck by the layout of the text. I noticed that the layout of the cookbook and the cricket text had some of the same features, including how-to sections, nutritional information, and images all on one page. Thus, the Do This, Not This Recipe activity was born.

Background

In order for students to see the connections between their academic lives and their personal ones, it is important for teachers to look for activities that can bridge the gap between the two. What better way to do this than to have students complete cookbooks and recipe cards? All students, regardless of whether they cook, will be familiar with this real-world format.

While this strategy contains a number of skills and content information, one of the most important components is the fact that it includes real-world examples as a bridge between the world and the classroom. Students need to list important information (ingredients) for each topic, write a procedural guide (steps), and utilize many of the key features of a recipe to complete this writing assignment.

Benefits

- This activity is flexible. You may elect to do this activity as a quick, informal assignment or as a more polished, formal one.

- This activity connects students to the real world.

- This activity is short and does not require extended writing.

Procedure

1. Locate concepts/topics specific to your discipline that have two opposing sides or multiple views.

2. Have students choose either a side of an issue or a component of the concept being addressed.

3. Provide time for students to conduct research on their chosen topic/issue using multiple sources.

4. Have students draft note cards modeled after the example texts used. **Note:** Each note card should have the following items: an image, information explaining the concept, pros and cons of the chosen topic, and other pertinent information.

Modifications

- Instead of note cards, have students each create one PowerPoint slide with the same required information (see page 114).

- Use a digital Internet tool such as Glogster to build the writing virtually.

Extensions

- Compile all the compositions into a class-made text.

- Use multiple note cards on the same topic to create a merged group product.

Content-Area Crossover

Regardless of the topic, students should include certain information modeled after the example texts. All cards should include:

- text features

- a persuasive element (Do This, Not That Recipe)

- graphics that enhance the text

- informational text about the topic

- key ideas

- Social Studies—Social studies offers a number of opportunities, such as political party choices, best historical leaders, and geographic regions to call home.

- Math—In math, students can choose to write about which strategies to use and which ones to avoid.

- Science—Science also offers a number of potential topics, including items such as genetic engineering, power sources, and environmental issues.

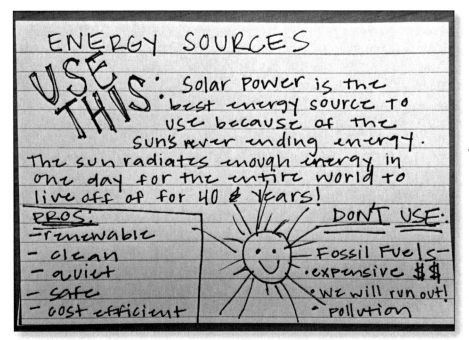

☆ This is a recipe note card for energy sources.

Create a Simile

Background

Students (at any age) are typically honest about which subjects they love or hate. This activity builds on these opinions to get students to write about their feelings and use evidence to support them.

One activity I have found that works is to have students create similes. Why? Because often, when students construct these types of comparisons, their choices for the similes reveal deeper opinions and perceptions. Knowing this information can give insight about attitudes and opinions regarding materials taught. For this activity, students need to support their simile with evidence and personal references.

Creating similes can serve as icebreakers or openers at the beginning of the semester/ unit, but they also work well throughout the year when major concepts or units are being studied.

Benefits

- This activity is abstract and critical in nature. It requires students to view items with a critical eye.

- This activity is low stakes and requires brief writing.

- This activity will interest students who like poetry.

Procedure

1. Provide students with a model of a simile.

2. Remind students of what a simile is.

Rock Star Tip

Make sure you model this activity first. Since it is one that is abstract in nature, students will probably need to see an actual example constructed.

3. Explain that students will create their own similes that follow the sentence frame: _____ *is like* _____ *because* _____.

4. Have students choose images, words, or phrases to create their own similes related to the subject or content.

Modifications

- Start with a general simile, and progress to a more specific one. For example, begin with, "Algebra is like _____ because _____." Then, move to one that is more specific, such as, "Linear equations are like _____ because _____."

Author's Thoughts

Once, when doing this activity, a student compared math to the show *Who Wants to Be a Millionaire.* Her sample stated that math was like the game show because there was only one final answer. Examining this answer gave me tremendous insight into how the student viewed math. I further questioned her about the process of solving problems in math and was told, "Oh, no...solving a problem is like basketball because there may be many different ways to score, but only one team (or answer) can win in the end."

Create a Simile *(cont.)*

- Students can add to the same picture as a group. Have them pass the same picture around and add their similes.

Extensions

- Use this activity as a way to review concepts for a summative assessment.

- Students will debate or defend their classmates' similes.

Content-Area Crossover

This activity can be easily modified for all content-area classrooms. For any subject, choose an appropriate topic to begin the prompt "_____ is like _____ because_____." Content teachers may be as specific or general as needed. For example, math teachers may complete this assignment with a general unit on decimals. However, this could also be used for something as specific as a genetic mutation in science classrooms.

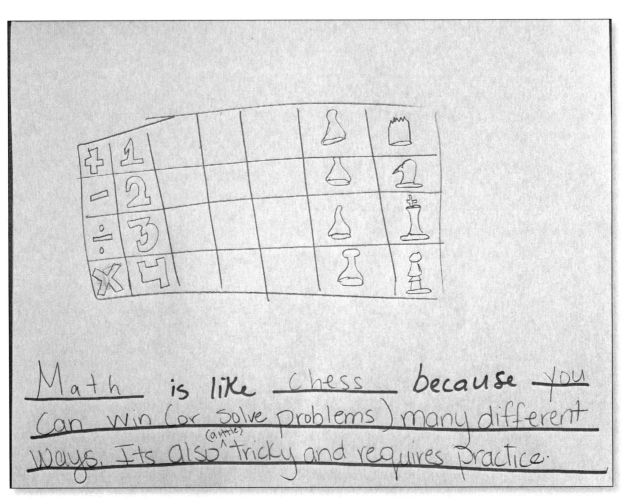

☆ This is an example of the Create a Simile activity conducted in a mathematics classroom.

© Shell Education

Continuum Debate

Background

Continuum Debates are great platforms for students to practice using evidence and facts to support their opinions. Students simply create oral arguments for one side of an issue. I often chose polarizing historical figures, events, or current issues.

This activity forces students to find, support, defend, and provide multiple examples to defend their opinions. Since the goal is to get their peers to their side of the argument (and classroom), arguments and positions must be strong and have weight and substance.

Benefits

- This activity contains movement breaks.

- The assignment is flexible in its degree of formality. Teachers may elect to do this as a quick, informal assignment or as a more polished, formal assignment.

- This activity allows students opportunities to practice listening and speaking.

- Students are actively thinking, comparing, justifying, and reviewing content-area material.

- Students are required to only include the most important events or ideas in their written argument.

Procedure

1. Pose the debate topic.

2. Give students time to think about which side they are on and to write a few key points to support their side of the issue.

3. Start with two students who have opposing views on either side of the classroom.

4. Give each student one minute to articulate his or her argument orally to the class. Once both students have done so, ask for other volunteers to place themselves on the imaginary line between the two students, based on how close they are to one side.

5. Allow the first two students who began the debate to add to their argument. Each volunteer standing on the imaginary line can then move based on whether they have been convinced by the students.

6. Continue this process for a few rounds before starting over the process with new volunteers.

Modifications

- If you are concerned about students being able to articulate and craft well-constructed paragraphs about their topics, modify them. Allow them to use their note cards to bullet-list their information instead of requiring them to write paragraphs. This modification can make the task more attainable for some students and may even serve as a time saver.

- What if your two debaters get stuck and can't think of additional information? Have them tag classmates to take their places.

> ### Rock Star Tip
> If you want to take out the competitive element, have individual students rate the debate at their desk. These reflections should be handed directly to the teacher.

Continuum Debate *(cont.)*

Extensions

- Use the Red-Light, Green-Light Evidence activity on page 40 to help students evaluate their evidence before debating.

- While the majority of this activity is oral and includes an abbreviated written format, teachers may choose to have students formally draft their arguments into fully developed argumentative pieces.

- Students from opposing sides should develop the counterclaims to present to their classmates with opposing compositions. Then, have them respond to the counterclaims presented by their classmates.

Content-Area Crossover

- Social Studies—There are many natural opportunities for this activity in the social studies classroom. For example, war strategies, political positions, and economic strategies are prime examples of debatable material.

- Math—Ever consider having a mathematical debate? Have students debate math concepts, different methods for solving the same problem, and deciding on effective strategies for gathering and displaying data.

- Science—Have students debate both sides of a controversial topic, such as genetically modified foods or animal testing.

iPod List

Background

Sometimes, content-area units of study can be very dense. When teaching, I try to think of ways to make concepts or figures interesting and exciting. One way to do this is to create an iPod List for characters, historical figures, or concepts.

This activity allows students to interact with topics in a more engaging (musical) way, and it gives them a chance to incorporate outside nonacademic knowledge into their classroom writing.

Benefits

- This activity capitalizes on student influences and interests.

- This activity integrates the arts.

- This activity involves short, succinct explanations of and justifications for the inclusion of chosen material.

Procedure

1. Determine the concept/content students will explore.

2. Have students create playlists of songs that could accompany the content. Make sure you set a specific number of songs you want included. **Note:** Students may be on this step for a few days or for the entire unit.

3. Give students materials and research resources to adequately find songs to fit their historical figures.

4. Have students develop a short rationale for each song included on the playlist. The template on page 117 can be used to present the list.

Modifications

- Instead of playlists, have students create soundtracks for novels, concepts, time periods, historical figures, or content units.

- Have students create playlists in a gallery walk. Post the concepts on chart paper for which playlists are being developed. Have students circulate the room and add songs to each concept.

Extensions

- Use the playlists to preview material. Instead of revealing the concept or person for whom the playlist was created, give the students the playlist and have them guess the topic.

- Allow students to continually add to the playlists as the year/unit progresses for especially dense and information-rich topics.

- Add images to student playlists. Have students create lists of images that could accompany specific songs. For example, what images would be on the CD case for the playlist generated?

- Burn students' playlists onto CDs, and have your next class listen to their selections and view their written rationales for each song.

Content-Area Crossover

While I used this mainly for historical figures, it could also be used for historical events, geographic regions, scientists, science concepts, math concepts, and more. This activity works well in all content-area classes.

Rock Star Tip

First, make sure to model this activity with the students. Have them listen to your rationale write-up and music selected before attempting to complete this activity. This model will showcase the written expectations and demonstrate the objectives for the iPod List activity.

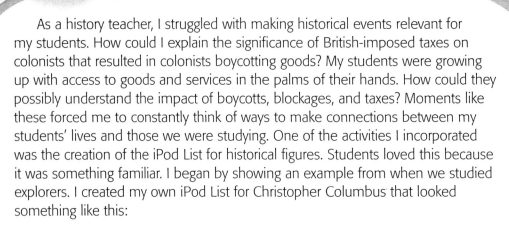

Author's Thoughts

As a history teacher, I struggled with making historical events relevant for my students. How could I explain the significance of British-imposed taxes on colonists that resulted in colonists boycotting goods? My students were growing up with access to goods and services in the palms of their hands. How could they possibly understand the impact of boycotts, blockages, and taxes? Moments like these forced me to constantly think of ways to make connections between my students' lives and those we were studying. One of the activities I incorporated was the creation of the iPod List for historical figures. Students loved this because it was something familiar. I began by showing an example from when we studied explorers. I created my own iPod List for Christopher Columbus that looked something like this:

Christopher Columbus's iPod Playlist

Track 1—"Sailing" by Christopher Cross

Track 2—"I Still Haven't Found What I'm Looking For" by U2

Track 3—"A Whole New World" (theme song from *Aladdin*) by Peabo Bryson and Regina Belle

When coming up with the title and artist for the first track, I thought about the beginning of Columbus's journey. When Columbus and his crew began their journey, that is exactly what they were doing: sailing. The second track is by the band U2. However, I thought it fit perfectly to explain the second leg of the expedition. Why? After Columbus and the crew had been on the ship sailing for a while, they were bored, discouraged, and disappointed. After all, this "new world" they were looking for still had not been found. Last, I channeled the crew's inner thoughts and decided to go with another familiar song. Why? Once Columbus and the crew found land, they realized that they could open up a whole new world to Europeans.

Writing to Learn Vocabulary

Vocabulary acquisition can be one of the most important components in a content-area classroom. Because students are required to read and write in each content area, an ample working vocabulary of Tier-Three words is necessary in order to effectively communicate both orally and written.

According to Baker, Simmons, and Kame'enui (1995, 7), "reading is probably the most important mechanism for vocabulary growth throughout a student's school years and beyond." However, many students, especially those who are developing readers and writers, do not read extensively enough to build large word banks. One strategy for the development of additional vocabulary is the use of word banks and word walls (Allen, 2000). However, Hilden and Jones (2012) warn teachers of potential pitfalls with this strategy, including the use of word walls as less of an instructional tool and more as classroom decoration. This section expands on the idea of word walls with activities that require students to post words for a purpose and add to the list throughout a unit.

Regardless of the activities used, the need for students to learn additional content-specific vocabulary is paramount. Students are surrounded by words on a daily basis—words that are both written and spoken. In order to be successful in all subject areas, students need to have opportunities to implement and use academic-specific words in their lives and in their daily writing.

Other activities in this section center around content-specific, or Tier-Three, words. Beck, McKeown, and Kucan's (2002) vocabulary research classifies words in a leveled tier system, with Tier-One words consisting of common, frequently used words, Tier-Two words including high-frequency words that can occur across contexts and disciplines, and Tier-Three words being more content-specific words. This tiered system can assist teachers in more purposeful vocabulary instruction. While much of this research addresses how and which types of words to teach explicitly, I argue that using components of the tiered system coupled with Maxwell's (1966) early research defining levels of writing based on format, audience, and function can offer additional benefits in the content-area classroom. Merging these two ideas helped me develop the Levels of Words activity (page 57). Because audience, format, and role are highly important in writing, they also are important in the acquisition and implementation of new vocabulary.

When I am teaching vocabulary lessons, I like to rank words by formality (academic vocabulary being the highest level). Level-One words are very informal. Examples include slang, abbreviations for common words and overused words, such as *good*, *bad*, and *sad*. Level-Two words are not quite as informal, but they have not reached the most formal academic stage. Words such as *image*, *vegetation*, and *vehicle* are the words that are in the middle. Level-Three words are the most sophisticated. Words such as *thesis*, *plethora*, and *antiquities* are examples of Level-Three words. In many cases, these are genre-specific words—words and phrases that are common to certain academic formats and papers. Often, these are the words that are discipline specific.

The strategies in this section focus on defining and stretching students' understanding of words (including synonyms and antonyms for vocabulary words). It is critical that students have a working, growing vocabulary, especially in the content-area classroom. The following strategies can be used as tools for building (and learning) vocabulary:

★ Levels of Words 57

★ Paint-Strip Words 59

★ Continuum of Words 61

★ Alpha-Boxes 63

★ Also Known As (AKA) 66

Levels of Words

Background

Using what we know about vocabulary words, this activity can be used in the content-area classroom to build academic vocabulary. Depending on the objective of the lesson, students can sort, use, and categorize words into levels based on their formality, length, or complexity. Students can also utilize this activity to house content-specific words learned during a unit, a semester, or a year for ongoing usage and study.

Benefits

- This activity is ongoing. Ideally, it could be used throughout the school year. You and your students should continue to add examples to each poster throughout the year.

- This activity encourages students to pay more attention to word structure, spelling, and grammar. Since students may use these words in their own writings, it is important that they use correct structure, spellings, and grammar.

Procedure

1. Create and label three posters for display in the classroom. They should read *Level-One Words*, *Level-Two Words*, and *Level-Three Words*.

2. Define each level, and provide a few examples of words for each.

3. Have students add their own suggestions and examples to the posters as the lesson or unit progresses. **Note:** As students encounter new words that fit on the posters, have them record and place the words on the appropriate posters.

Modifications

- For primary students, consider changing the titles of the posters to better suit your students' needs. For example, change the labels to *High-Frequency Words* or *Words I Can't Sound Out*. For this population, consider integrating images as well. This may help some students who have difficulty reading.

- One way to seamlessly integrate vocabulary teaching is to keep a pocket chart of newly acquired vocabulary displayed in your classroom. You can also keep a "parking lot" of words displayed in your room. The parking lot simply includes sticky notes attached to chart paper with new words. If you start with a general parking lot in the beginning of the year, revisit your lot toward the middle of the year, and attempt to sort the words into levels. For the rest of the year, students should use, label, and add to the leveled parking lot as they come across new vocabulary words.

Extensions

- Encourage students to use the Levels of Words Template (page 113) to create personal word lists. The lists can be referenced during speaking or writing assignments to encourage use of Level-Two and Level-Three words.

- Have students justify why they placed a word in a specific level.

- When revising and editing, encourage students to "level up" and swap lower-level words for higher-level words.

Rock Star Tip

Take it slow. It is easy to move students from a Level-One word to a Level-Two word. It is harder to move them from a Level-One word straight to a Level-Three word.

- Try leveling down! Take a denser academic passage and have students substitute some Level-Three words with Level-Two or Level-One words.

- Use the template on page 113 as an individual level charts for students to use at their desks. They can be tailored specifically to the students or the task. This can assist students who are on a variety of reading and writing levels because, while some words will be the same for all, each students will have some words that are exclusive to their learning needs.

Content-Area Crossover

- Social Studies—In the social studies classroom, students can use the Levels of Words activity to define era-specific historical words, leveling them down to modern, informal words we use today.

- Math—In math, have students sort words into levels, and use this list when explaining how they solved problems. Instead of writing *I added to get my answer,* push students to write *I used addition to compute and find the sum.*

Author's Thoughts

Students are most versed in the words of their worlds. Some time ago, I met with some eighth grade teachers who were lamenting that their students were not using the vocabulary words taught during class in their own conversations and writing. Many of them were concerned that students were not transferring the words taught in ELA class into their own discussions.

When I asked which words they were studying, they gave me words such as *agile, aloof,* and *banter.* What eighth grade students do you know who use those words in their everyday speech? Better yet, what adults do you know who use those words on a regular basis? It is highly unlikely that you will encounter a conversation at a middle school lunch table that involves one student saying to another, "You were awfully agile on the field yesterday." "You seem a little aloof today. Is everything OK?" Rarely, will you hear a middle school student speak this way. The importance, I explained, was that these students should be able to effectively use these words in their *academic* writing.

Paint-Strip Words

Background

When students write about discipline-specific content or write compositions in distinctive genres, there are certain vocabulary words that should be employed in the compositions and responses. Often, teachers have specific phrases, transition words, or genre- and content-area-specific words that they want used in these compositions. One way to assist students with a visual reminder of these words is to use paint strips that include the words that should be used in the composition.

This personalized (nonnegotiable) list allows students to have word banks at their fingertips. This activity can be differentiated based on students' assignments, content, or ability level. Plus, students can store these lists in pocket charts in the classroom to use as needed throughout the academic year.

Benefits

- This activity is short and focused.

- This activity is easily differentiated. Each list is tailored to the task and objectives for completing the writing.

- This activity can be used several times during the school year.

- This activity can be completed in class, at home, with partners, or as a needs-based activity for students who need reference documents to help them with their writings.

Rock Star Tip

Don't have paint strips? Sentence strips or construction paper cut into strips will do the job, or you can utilize the template on page 115. The most important component is that all strips are divided so students can organize ideas.

Procedure

1. Determine the appropriate paint-strip configuration that will best suit your lesson objectives. (See page 115 for a paint-strip template.)

2. Give students specific directions for completing the strips. For example, if they are supposed to locate a certain number of words from a certain source, make sure the instructions are explicit enough for students to do so.

3. Determine if there are any nonnegotiable words or phrases that *must* be included on the strips.

4. Give instructions for any additional information that should be included. For example, let students know if you want them to include the sources where they found the words or if you want them to locate that content-specific word in their texts somewhere.

Modifications

- Modify the length of the paint strip based on students' needs.

- Give students some (or all) of the focus words. Scaffold the lesson every time you complete it by giving students fewer teacher-determined nonnegotiable words.

- Use paint strips to help students remember the order, sequence, or steps for a project, task, or procedure.

Extensions

- Younger students can go on a word scavenger hunt using their paint strips to house found words.

- When completing an extended response later in the unit, have students refer to the paint strips to help construct their responses.

Content-Area Crossover

- Social Studies—Paint strips can be used in any content area that requires students to use content-specific vocabulary in their writing. This activity is especially beneficial in the social studies class because the visual representation allows students to center and focus their work using front-loaded new or task-specific vocabulary words.

- Math—You can use these paint strips to list essential words needed when explaining and writing about mathematical thinking. Explaining the steps of a multi-step word problem or a geometric proof.

- Science—In the science class, allow students to keep a running record of vocabulary words learned in each lesson. Later, they can use these words when writing longer pieces or jot down a student-friendly definition for an individual unit dictionary.

- Art—In art, Paint-Strip Words can be used to collect the names of artists who composed in specific artistic styles. Use the list later for larger research projects or as a reference for classroom discussions.

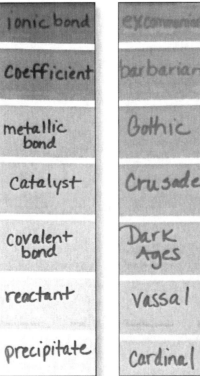

☆ Here are some paint-strip vocabulary words from chemistry and social studies classes.

Continuum of words

Author's Thoughts

One of the best parts of this activity is the conversation that comes out of it. Students are able to articulate and defend why a certain word should be placed somewhere along a continuum. They are able to make arguments and are forced to support these arguments based on what they know about the words in their daily lives and from content-area lessons and materials.

Background

This activity helps students learn words with similar meanings. Like the activity Also Known As (page 66), students identify synonyms and practice using words with similar meanings.

This activity is especially beneficial to English language learners because they are taught multiple words that can be represented by one word. In addition, students are taught the subtle nuances between familiar words, which can expand their academic vocabularies. For example, the words *scary*, *frightening*, *chilling*, *creepy*, *horrifying*, and *spooky* have similar definitions. Each word, however, has a slight variance in meaning and severity.

Benefits

- This activity includes movement breaks.

- This activity provides another opportunity for students to learn new words and build academic vocabulary.

- This activity promotes class discussion.

Procedure

1. Choose five to seven words that fit on a continuum.

2. Write each word on a note card.

3. Distribute note cards with words and blank ones.

4. Have students with the word cards arrange themselves in a line based on your directive. For example, you may choose to have students arrange themselves in order of least scary to scariest emotion, or you may ask them to arrange themselves based on how formal or informal the words are.

5. Invite the rest of the class to offer suggestions about the word lineup. Have them direct the selected students on how they should rearrange themselves, if needed.

6. After repeating step 5 a few times, have students who were not selected use the blank note cards to add new words to the Continuum of Words.

7. Repeat steps 5 and 6 as needed.

Modifications

- If you are worried about having too many students up at one time or if space is an issues, start small. Give students a paint strip to use at their desks (see page 115).

- Give and display the words that you want students to arrange.

- For students struggling with reading and writing, provide prewritten cards. Use blank cards for accelerated students or those who may be more comfortable adding new words to the continuum.

Extensions

- Students can use this activity as a springboard to longer, more detailed writing.

- Have students create images to go with their continuum, paying close attention to the subtle differences between each word.

- Consider using this activity as a time line.

Rock Star Tip

Challenge students to work on their nonverbal communication skills and complete the activity without talking.

Students can use the same procedures and organize themselves in chronological order.

Content-Area Crossover

This activity can be modified in a content-area lesson that requires student to see the subtle nuances in things, be it shades in art, scientific words, or historical events in social studies. Conversely, you may opt to use this activity to showcase events, topics, and ideas that build upon each other in any content-area classroom.

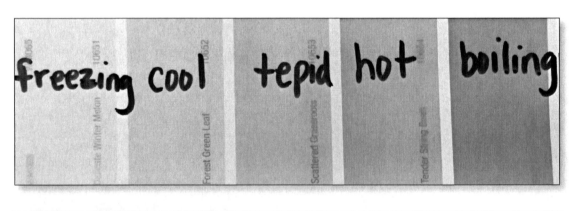

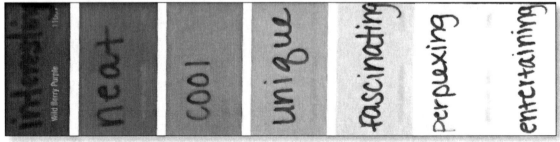

☆ Here are two paint-strip variations of the Continuum of Words activity.

Alpha-Boxes

Background

Alpha-Boxes can aid in vocabulary acquisition and activate students' prior knowledge in the content-area classroom. This activity is easy to use and can be used at the beginning, during, or as a culminating activity for a content-area unit.

For this activity, students have to make word associations for a content-specific topic. Encourage students to get creative and use words, sketches, or phrases to make as many associations as possible. This activity stretches and expands students' understanding of a given topic.

Benefits

- This activity can be used as an ongoing formative assessment.

- This activity requires participation from you and students, promoting a two-way-street model of learning.

- This activity promotes classroom discussion.

- Use this strategy at the beginning of a unit to activate prior knowledge—something crucial for comprehension and an added benefit for English language learners (ELLs).

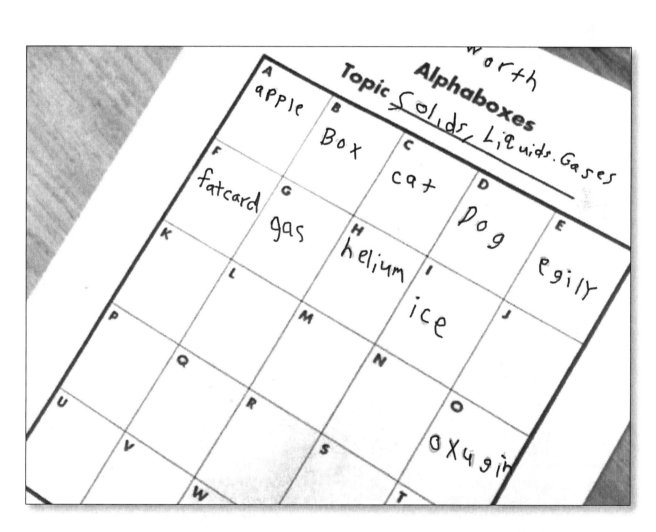

☆ This Alpha-Box activity was completed in an elementary education science classroom.

Procedure

1. Have students write each letter of the alphabet on a sheet of paper, leaving space for writing words under each letter (or use the template on page 108).

2. Write the theme or topic above the Alpha-Box. To complete the activity, each associated word needs to start with the letter under which it is being placed. For example, if the topic is wars that shaped the United States of America, under the letter /W/, students can list *War of 1812,* and under the letter /C/, they can list *Civil War.*

3. Provide time for students to share their activity sheets with the class. Clarify any misconceptions or incorrect vocabulary words. Allow students to add words that they may have missed.

Modifications

- To use Alpha-Boxes throughout a unit, have students add words to their lists daily. As they learn more content, more words go in each box. This activity should be viewed as a running list—one that can be added to and taken from as students clarify understanding of a topic.

- To use Alpha-Boxes as a culminating activity, have students fill in their words after completing a unit.

- If 26 letters seem too overwhelming for students, have them circle or star only a few letters at first. This may help them focus on a few letters rather than all of them.

- If students need fewer letters to focus on, consider giving a range of letters to aim for throughout the activity. This allows students the flexibility of using the letters that they feel are the strongest, removing the daunting task of assigning all 26 letters.

- Create a large Alpha-Boxes chart in the classroom that students can add to during any giving unit, semester, or year. This works well in primary classrooms, since some students may not know how to write or spell the words yet.

Extensions

- When finished, you can leave the Alpha-Boxes as they are, or you can use them as springboards to other activities. For example, you may elect to have students choose one letter each from their Alpha-Boxes sheets to create a page for a picture book. Since each student would have his or her own letter to write about and illustrate, the class will be able to assemble an entire alphabet picture book about a given topic.

- Assign a number of letters to extend writing, and have students use their Alpha-Boxes sheets to write sentences about the chosen letters.

Content-Area Crossover

- Social Studies—Alpha-Boxes are handy for activities that require students to use vocabulary and lists. In the social studies class, use Alpha-Boxes to list and identify character traits of historical figures, important terms for a historical period, or events that were important to certain groups of people or regions.

> ### Rock Star Tip
> On a consistent basis—daily or weekly—have students share what they've added to their Alpha-Boxes. This gives classmates time to add words that they may have missed and allows you to clarify misconceptions or incorrectly placed words.

Alpha-Boxes *(cont.)*

- Math—In mathematics, use an Alpha-Box to label key mathematical words, terms, or concepts after teaching a unit.

- Science—In science, use two Alpha-Boxes to have students compare concepts. For example, you may have students work with partners to fill in one activity listing only living things and another activity listing nonliving things.

- Art—In art, use this activity to have students combine materials (charcoal, paint, or colored pencils) to invent new colors and name them.

Aorta	Brain / bicep	Cranium	Digits / dorsal
Egg / elbow / endocrine	Femur / fallopian	Gall bladder	Heart
Intestines	Jugular / joints	K	Liver
Mammary glands	Nose / nervous system	Ovary	Patella / phalanges
Quadricept	R	Stomach	Thyroid / throat
U ulna / uterus	V	W	XYZ / zygote

ANATOMY
Alpha-Boxes

☆ This activity was completed in a secondary education science classroom.

Also Known As (AKA)

Background

All too often, one word on a test can mean the difference between students answering a question correctly or incorrectly. The difference between *read the excerpt of the text* and *read the passage* may seem like a small difference, but to some students, it is huge.

One activity to extend students' understanding of words and phrases is the Also Known As (AKA) activity. This activity develops a word bank for content-specific words and their synonyms. This chart can be added to throughout the year. It helps to cast the vocabulary net a bit wider since students are no longer confined to using one word for a concept or a behavior. Instead, students learn numerous words as suitable substitutes. For example, students may have learned the word *solution* as it relates to a mathematical answer. It is important, however, that students understand that *solution* can be used interchangeably with the words *answer, product, result, sum, conclusion, difference,* and *quotient.*

Benefits

- This activity is ongoing. Ideally, it should be used multiple times throughout the school year.

- This activity will appeal to the visual learner.

- This activity builds academic vocabulary.

- This activity will benefit English language learners.

Procedure

1. Display a T-chart labeled *Also Known As* or *AKA*.

2. Provide a few examples of words to start the chart.

3. Encourage students to offer additions to the chart when they encounter other words that fit with the list of words.

Modifications

- Instead of using this chart as a means to help with test taking and academic vocabulary expansion, have students use it to offer substitutes for overused words.

- Use this activity with a stem/root/affix activity so that students can see how certain roots/stems/affixes occur in multiple academic settings.

- Use an AKA chart before starting a unit or lesson. This will elicit what students know about a given topic. Revisit the chart once the lesson is complete to add any additional learning students may have had.

Extensions

- Have students go on a scavenger hunt to locate additional words that can be added to the chart.

- Have students rewrite word problems and constructed response prompts using different synonyms from the chart.

 Drumming for More

Need an archive of roots and stems? Try the Learn That Word website (learnthat.org). This site has a section devoted to roots, stems, and affixes.

Content-Area Crossover

Every content area has discipline-specific words that can be represented in multiple ways. Any content-area classroom can use this activity for multi-meaning words or synonyms. Because this type of chart focuses more on vocabulary, you may elect to use these charts in addition to word walls already displayed in their classes. For English language learners, a visual AKA chart displayed in the classroom can help with word acquisition and reinforce academic vocabulary.

Author's Thoughts

Several years ago, my family was vacationing in Chicago. During this time, one of the *Transformers* movies was being filmed in downtown Chicago, complete with helicopters, mangled cars and roads, and BASE jumpers who leapt from building to building. One afternoon while we were walking through the sets, my daughters asked what *transformers* were, to which we replied, "They are alien robots." (Truly, that was the easiest explanation within the context of the movie.)

This exchange was so brief that I didn't even consider it important until months later, when we were home and our power went out. When my daughter asked me why we lost power, I told her that a transformer probably blew up. The look on her face was part puzzled, part bewildered, part horrified. She asked me once more, and I repeated my answer, to which she asked, "We get our power from aliens?"

Now, what does this have to do with vocabulary? Everything! You see, the only concept my daughter had of the word *transformer* was the definition I had provided her in Chicago. In her world, she didn't know that the word had multiple meanings. For her, it was static and fixed and meant one thing: "an alien robot."

Now, think about your students. The same thing happens to them when they encounter a word that they have never seen before or they have learned only one definition for. Unfortunately, when this happens, students can miss the entire message of a question or a piece of writing because of that one word. Sadly, this is not something that happens only to young students. It happens to all of us at some point.

Writing to Summarize

The ability to summarize material in all disciplines is an important skill. Regardless of the discipline, many standards include components that mandate that students condense, synthesize, summarize, and write about material. However, for some students, this is a challenge. In fact, Berke and Woodland (1995) indicate that "no greater challenge to the intellect and no more accurate test of understanding exist than the ability to contemplate an idea and then restate it briefly in your own words" (370). Summarizing content requires that students divulge what they have taken away from the material in an organized, brief manner.

This section includes a variety of strategies that can be used to teach the skill of summarizing. Many of the activities capitalize on social media influences and modern student interests. The following strategies can be used as tools for summarizing:

★ Postcard Summaries 69

★ Sports Summaries 71

★ Trailers, Recap, and Reviews 73

★ Five-Dollar Summaries 75

★ Comic-Strip Summaries 77

★ Bio Poems 2.0 79

★ Social Media Summaries 81

Postcard Summaries

Background

People who send postcards understand the importance of summarization. Because postcards are relatively small, writers have to determine what key highlights should be included.

Postcards offer teachers opportunities to teach the skill of summarization. For example, incorporating an image on the opposite side of the text allows students to explore the artistic nature of summarization. Students should ask themselves: *What picture should be chosen to best capture the main idea of the trip? What words are crucial in summarizing their thoughts? What words can be omitted?*

Benefits

- This activity appeals to visual learners.

- Postcard Summaries can serve as brief or extended activities.

- Students practice writing in letter/note format and use formal writing based on audience.

- This strategy includes a visual component. This offers students opportunities to represent ideas visually in addition to traditional academic writing.

Procedure

1. Show examples of completed postcards. Draw attention to the structure of the text, brevity, and details included on the back of the card.

2. Display and discuss the pictures on the front of the postcards.

3. Provide students with blank note cards on which to write their postcard summaries.

4. On the front of the card, have students draw pictures that best represent the concept or idea being summarized. On the back of the card, have students write summaries about the topics discussed and address them to a friend.

Modifications

- Instead of having students create summaries of material, have them practice matching prewritten summaries to postcard pictures. This can help assist students in creating their own images or words for their summaries later.

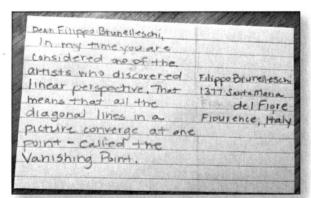 

☆ This is a sample of a Postcard Summary conducted in a mathematics classroom.

- Try "peer postcard" summaries. With this modification, students begin to construct postcards about a concept and then swap postcards at predetermined times. They stop writing on their cards and pick up where a peer left off on another card.

Extensions

- While the main point of this activity is for students to construct short summaries, postcards can also serve as springboards to longer, more extensive writing pieces.

- Extend writing and have each student become postcard buddies with another student. Have students correspond together several times throughout the school year.

Content-Area Crossover

- Social Studies—Postcard Summaries can be used in all subject areas and are the perfect vehicle for inserting creativity into all concepts and topics. In the social studies class, have students include historical images, photographs, or images to represent their postcard summary (this may require research). Students could write Postcard Summaries from historical figures, summarizing key historical events or battles, geographic region recaps, and more.

- Math—Similar to the social studies suggestion, have students use diagrams, graphs, or models of math problems as postcard images. Or, have students write postcards to friends outlining the key components of functions.

- Science—Use Postcard Summaries as an assessment tool. Instead of giving formal assessments, students can use Postcard Summaries to reflect on the content learned, including illustrations to visually represent the topic. Science teachers could use them after a number of units, including those on genetics, biomes, and more. Plus, Postcard Summaries could be used to review components of larger, denser units that include a number of moving parts and that build upon each other.

- Art—Use works of art already studied in class as springboards to written summaries (or descriptions) of collections of art or specific movements. The same can apply to music, as students could summarize specific genres of music, use sheet music as images, and complete written summaries that provide overviews of the piece.

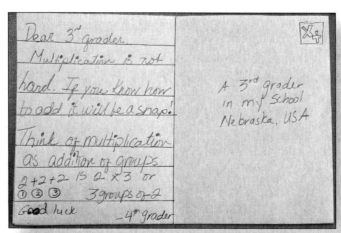

☆ **This Postcard Summary was completed in an elementary education math classroom.**

Sports Summaries

Author's Thoughts

I am not the person anyone comes to when they want to discuss sports. However, I spend a lot of time in the same room with my husband while he watches a variety of athletic events. It was on one of these occasions that I realized that sports-highlights reels are meaningful vehicles for teaching written summaries.

Background

A Sports Summary is a unique way to incorporate sports into the content-area lesson. The focus of this summary is to highlight the most important information in a short amount of time (similar to a sports commentator).

When you watch the highlights from a game, the commentators don't show the entire game. They only show the most pivotal moments, the key events in the game. The focus is not on the 20 minutes when the offense only gained a few yards, but instead it is on touchdowns, interceptions, fumbles, game-changing calls, and injuries. In other words, it is a summary of the game, quarter, half, or period.

Benefits

- This activity will interest students who like, watch, and play sports.

- The summaries can serve as brief or extended activities, depending on time.

Procedure

1. Determine the sports-highlights reel you will use as an introduction to the strategy.

2. Instruct students to pay close attention to the length of time of the recap, the information included, the key plays, etc.

3. Provide students with the material they will be summarizing.

4. As a class, discuss a few of the "key plays" of the text, topic, or unit they are reviewing.

5. Have students write a summary. If time permits have students present their summaries to the class.

Modification

- Are you worried that your students may not be able to summarize the material without the help of a more concrete list of what to include? Give them a list of sports-related terms for concepts that need to be included, such as key players (characters/figures), key plays (important events, plot), major upsets (conflict, turning points), and fumbles (things that went wrong along the way). Lists like this may help students pinpoint what should be included.

Sports Summaries *(cont.)*

Extensions

- Have students present their summaries to the class.

- Have students use video tools such as iMovie® to record their summaries and enhance them with music and digital effects.

- Have students work with partners or groups to cover a large unit or several events.

Content-Area Crossover

- Social Studies—Use Sports Summaries to describe pivotal battles, wars, movements, or historical figures or events.

- Math—Use this strategy to summarize the way a problem was solved for a major unit of study. Make this an interactive presentation, and have students pair up to present. One student will read a script detailing how to solve a problem, while the other one works out the problem in real time in front of the class.

- Science—Summarize key scientific advances and discoveries, describe scientists being studied, or other science concepts and units of study.

☆ These students are presenting their Sports Summaries in front of their social studies classmates.

© *Shell Education*

Trailers, Recaps, and Reviews

Background

Think about a movie trailer. Production companies do a superb job of compressing feature-length movies into two-and-a-half-minute trailers that capture enough of the movie for viewers to get solid ideas of what the movies are about without having to watch the whole thing. Trailers do not give away the resolutions or pivotal components of movies. However, in order for trailers to be effective, they must provide adequate information so that viewers are aware of the basic characters, plots, and problems of the movies. With the exception of resolutions, movie trailers are excellent examples of summaries in the real world.

A similar example is an episode recap for a television show. When new episodes air for shows that have continuous plots, the new episodes are typically preceded by recaps of the prior week's shows. In this recap, only the key events that are needed to understand the forthcoming episode are shown.

On reality shows with a live finale, networks often play up the last show by showing a special episode prior to the finale. This review episode is dedicated to summarizing the entire season. The audiences get to see the dramatic highs and lows of the season before the final competition or big crowning.

How could you use Trailers, Recaps, and Reviews in your classroom? The simplest way is to use them as visual examples of what summaries could look like. However, you could take it a step further by having students create quick video clips, trailers, or scripts of specific concepts or material that they have addressed in class.

Benefits

- This activity will interest students who like to watch movies.

- This activity has the potential to include artistic and design elements if students elect to create their own digital trailers or storyboards.

- This activity requires multiple skills; students need to speak, listen, take notes, and write.

Procedure

1. Choose the type of summary most appropriate for the task. Model the attributes for this type of summary. **Note:** When using trailers and recaps as examples, you should ask students to identify the key features of each format. What components are necessary to include in the trailer or recap in order for it to be effective? What information is left out? Why? What words are they using? Do these summaries follow a specific sequence or order? Are characters identified?

2. Show students a movie trailer, a show recap, or portions of a review episode as a model. Make sure students take notes regarding the key features of each format.

3. Have students write scripts for their trailers, recaps, or reviews.

Modifications

- Instead of a written summary, have students construct a storyboard with pictures of the key components.

- Use graphic organizers or lists as frameworks for students to identify specific components of the material. For example, you might ask students to list the key characters, plot, pivotal moments, etc.

Trailers, Recaps, and Reviews *(cont.)*

- Lack the technology to do this activity digitally? Have students use hard copies of images to create a cut-and-paste version of a storyboard or a trailer.

Extensions

- Show products created by students in other classes, and have them guess which event is being summarized.

- What if you gave each group of students a concept or unit and required them to create a movie trailer or sitcom recap of the material? Your classes could complete an end-of-the-year review that would help them remember key information prior to the state assessments.

Content-Area Crossover

- Social Studies—Use the Trailers, Recaps, and Reviews summary to create a review of the content, such as key battles, historical periods, or industrial advances.

- Math—Trailers, Recaps, and Reviews could serve as great reminder for a unit. They also could be used as a means of explaining the computations and processes for completing problems.

- Science—Recap a unit on force and motion, using one of the summary formats. Turn this into a full presentation by assigning students objectives, guidelines, and rubrics for showcasing their understanding.

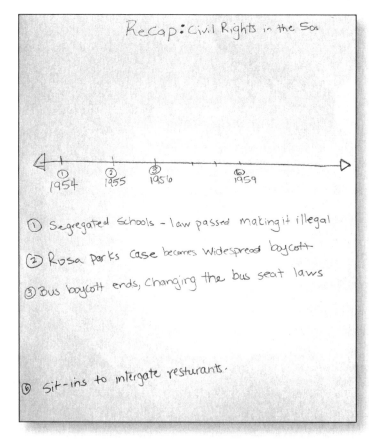

☆ This is an example of a Recap conducted in a social studies classroom.

51560—Content-Area Writing That Rocks (and Works!) © Shell Education

Five-Dollar Summaries

Background

Sometimes when students construct summaries, they include extraneous information. Five-Dollar Summaries can be used across content areas to help students identify key details and guide them to crafting more concise summaries. By assigning specific dollar amounts for each summary, students are able to see exactly how much material and how many words or sentences are required to complete the activity.

Benefits

- This activity will interest students who enjoy playful rules and challenges.

- This activity incorporates basic mathematics and computation skills.

- This activity requires students to pay close attention to word count and details.

Procedure

1. Assign a monetary value to each word or sentence (display this information in the classroom as an easy reference for students). For example, if each word were assigned a value of 10¢, then the summary could include no more than 50 words.

2. Instruct students to complete summaries that total no more than $5.00. **Note:** You can vary the assigned monetary value based on the material students are summarizing. (In this case, have students complete three-dollar or ten-dollar summaries instead.)

Modification

- Distribute play paper money and coins in a variety of denominations. Have each student write his or her summary based on the amount of money he or she received. This will allow teachers to target varying ability levels without singling out differentiations to students and/or the class as a whole.

Extensions

- Extend this lesson to have students compile multiple summaries to make $20.00 essays (or another monetary value).

- Shorten the writing by having students create 50¢ main idea sentences from their Five-Dollar Summaries.

Content-Area Crossover

- Social Studies—Change the activity to a Five-Dollar Biography. In this modification, assign monetary values to each biographical detail students research when studying historical figures. This ensures that students include the pertinent information but keeps the activity brief.

- Math—Adjust the total amount when there is less material to summarize. When summarizing an entire unit, teachers may increase the dollar amount so that students include all the needed material. Conversely, if you want a short snapshot of your students' understanding, you can lower the amount of the summary.

> **Rock Star Tip**
>
> This skill reinforces mathematics computation skills and allows students to self-monitor their word choice when constructing a summary.

- Science—Assign monetary values to each component of a lab report. Allot more money if students want or need to add images, charts, or visual proof of their thinking.

- Art—Similar to the social studies example, assign monetary value to each fact and detail included in a written report. Make the project interesting by having students use illustrations and graphics, assigning these monetary values as well.

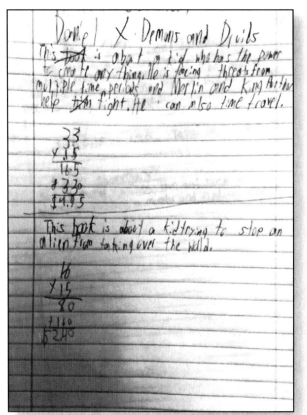

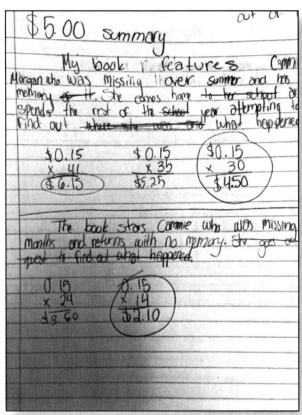

☆ Here are few examples of Five-Dollar Summaries.

Comic-Strip Summaries

Background

Comic strips and graphic novels have returned to popularity in recent years. Storyboards and comic strips are ways to visually summarize information. This artistic activity requires students to capture the overall content of a lesson and summarize it complete with images and text. Comic-Strip Summaries are especially beneficial for struggling or reluctant readers and writers. For this activity, students do not rely solely on the words to construct the meaning of a story. Instead, they are able to use pictures and graphics to assist them when summarizing their thoughts.

Because images play a significant role in students' lives outside of school (Kress and van Leeuwen 1996), teachers can use images to assist in making connections and aid in comprehension of material inside of school (Park 2012). Integrating comic strips and graphic novels capitalizes on this knowledge.

Benefits

- This activity capitalizes on student interest (graphic novels and comics).

- This activity will interest artistic students.

- This activity will appeal to the reluctant writer.

Procedure

1. Model the task for students (panels, writing expectations, etc.).

2. Provide students with blank comic-strip frames with a specific number of panels. Each panel represents an important detail or idea from the material.

3. Ask students to determine what main components to include.

4. Have students write one detail as a caption in each panel on the blank comic strips.

5. Direct students to illustrate each panel.

Modifications

- Use paint strips instead of blank comic strips.

- Differentiate by assigning some students strips with more or fewer panels.

- Instead of captions at the bottom of each panel, have students use dialogue and thought bubbles to summarize material.

Extensions

- Have students extend the Comic-Strip Summary to create comic books or graphic novels.

- Allow students to create peer comic strips, comic books, or graphic novels. Pairing students with classmates who are strong artists or strong writers can help support students in creating final products.

- Once students have created the storyboards or comic strips, cut them into individual panels and use them for sequencing and organizing or for stretching a story by adding additional panels with new details.

Rock Star Tip

Prepare comic strips beforehand. Differentiate the length, frame, writing lines, and spacing of each comic strip for individual students. This step will help target students' learning needs/styles in the classroom.

Content-Area Crossover

- Social Studies—Incorporate Comic-Strip Summaries when studying historical figures as a means of unpacking difficult primary sources, materials, or political cartoons.

- Math—Use Comic-Strip Summaries to showcase the steps and/or sequences used when solving mathematical problems. This activity can even be used as an exit ticket to recap daily lessons.

- Science—Use comic strips for lab safety reminders, lab reports, and with units that include visual components, diagrams, or figures. These summaries can also be used for showing the process of natural occurrences or experiments.

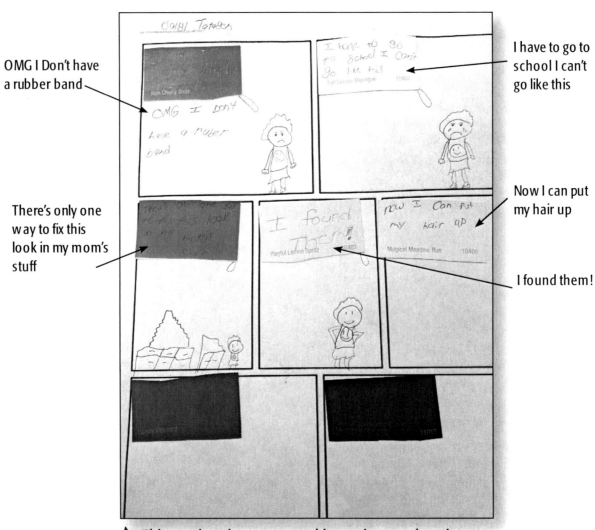

OMG I Don't have a rubber band

I have to go to school I can't go like this

There's only one way to fix this look in my mom's stuff

Now I can put my hair up

I found them!

☆ This comic strip was created in a primary education classroom.

Bio Poems 2.0

Author's Thoughts

Despite the fact that my students liked Bio Poems, I loathed them. After using them for a few years I tossed the Bio Poem template to the side with no plans of ever using it again. However, the more I thought about it, the more I realized that I needed to stop hating Bio Poems. They had their place, after all, but where?

That is when I realized they worked beautifully in the content-area classroom (with modification). I began to use them in my social studies classes for historical figures and battles. My students gravitated to the new template structure, and I realized they were great vehicles for writing summaries.

Background

Bio Poems are traditionally used in classes for students to write information about themselves. In fact, many teachers use these at the beginning of the year as a way of getting to know their students. These poems are formulaic and typically include prompts that require students to include specific information about themselves in poem format. Because the prompts are fairly straightforward, they are often easy for students to complete, as length and content are predetermined. While their original purpose was for students to construct writing pieces about themselves, they are wonderful venues for content-area writing.

Bio Poems 2.0 have the same objectives. Students write character traits and summarize; however, in Bio Poems 2.0, students are not required to only write about themselves or characters in a text.

Benefits

- This activity will interest students who like to read, write, and listen to poetry.

- The sentence frames provide scaffolds to support reluctant writers.

- This activity require students to conduct research. There is a format for students to follow so that research is focused and organized.

- This activity is low stakes.

- This activity elicits interesting information about a number of topics.

Procedure

1. Provide students with Bio Poem 2.0 templates (see page 110).

3. Provide materials, technology, and time for students to conduct research on a topic.

4. Have students use their research to complete a Bio Poem 2.0.

Bio Poems 2.0 *(cont.)*

Modifications

- Instead of writing the Bio Poems 2.0 on paper, have students write them on sentence strips. Differentiate the length of the sentence strip for students who are reluctant writers.

- Have students complete a collaborative Bio Poem 2.0. Each student is responsible for certain sections of the poem.

Extensions

- Use this activity as a springboard to a larger research piece.

- Have students compile multiple poems about the same topic and compare the research material found.

Content-Area Crossover

Research writing seems to be one of the most difficult types to master for some students. However, the act of conducting research, locating sources, paraphrasing, citing sources, etc., is an important skill in all content-area classrooms. This type of activity gives students the opportunity to practice research on a smaller scale before moving on to larger projects such as research papers. With that said, Bio Poems 2.0 will work well in all content-area classrooms. They are fairly short compositions, they can be integrated into any lessons, and they serve as a stand-alone activity.

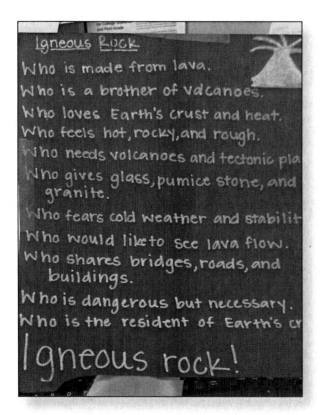

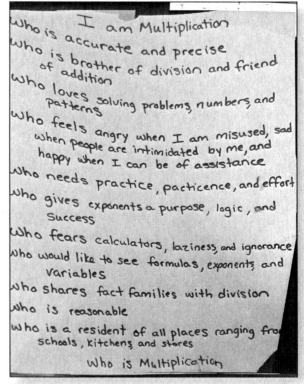

☆ These Bio Poems 2.0 samples were created in science and mathematics classrooms.

© Shell Education

Social Media Summaries

Background

One way to address the skill of summarizing is by using social media influences. Because many students are fluent in using social media, (hashtags, Instagram®, and/or tweets) Social Media Summaries are engaging ways to get students to interact with content-specific material.

While there are several social media examples for this skill, tweets and Instagram captions are fantastic vehicles for initiating Social Media Summaries. These summaries can be used as hooks for lessons or as the actual product you want students to create.

Benefits

- This activity will interest students who like and use social media.

- This activity is informal.

- Students are encouraged to apply their informal communication skills in an academic context.

Procedure for Hashtag Summaries

1. Introduce students to hashtag summaries. Explain the main purpose of a hashtag summary (to summarize the material into a word or a short phrase).

2. Model some hashtag summaries.

3. Give students time to think of an overarching hashtag that summarizes the message or main idea of the material taught. The template on page 116 can be used to present students final Hashtag Summaries.

4. Ask students to share their Hashtag Summaries.

5. In a longer unit or lesson, create a classroom display of all hashtags for later use and review.

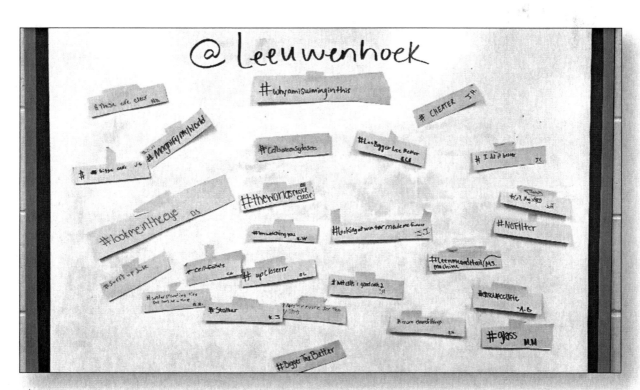

☆ This image shows how hashtags are used in a science classroom.

Author's Thoughts

Last year, I went to my daughter's third grade classroom and observed some summertime selfies hanging outside the classroom. Each student had drawn a picture of his or her summer activity on a template of a smartphone and had written a tweet about their summer fun. As I looked at the selfies, I noticed that some students had included a hashtag with their tweets. For example, in the image below, one student included #charlestonfun.

☆ This Hashtag Summary is from a third grade classroom.

Think about the example above. The hashtag related to the overarching main idea of the summertime selfie drawing and tweet. In other words, this student wrote about his summer escapades and then encapsulated them in a hashtag that functioned as a main idea, thus effectively summarizing the event in one word or phrase.

I began to think about this. If students as young as third grade know enough about hashtags to know that they can function as main ideas, why not use them in teaching? As a result, I began using this idea to teach summarization and main idea.

Social Media Summaries (cont.)

Procedure for Summaries as Tweets

1. Explain that students will summarize using 140 characters or less (including spaces). **Note:** You may need to explain what a 'character' is to some students.

2. Show students sample tweets.

3. Have students summarize the material using tweets. Have students check their character count before submitting their tweets.

Modifications

- Have students complete a series of tweets as a group. Have each group member write a tweet that captures the main idea of the lesson. Once this is done, group members can discuss their responses and any commonalities noted.

- Use various types of text for each topic. Assign groups different texts that center around specific themes. For example, when studying climate change, several articles may be used. One group may receive a passage regarding climate change and the effects on a specific region. Another group may read about the causes of climate change. Yet another group may read a graph that explains climate change in a more visual way. The type and number of materials used are completely up to you and should be based on the unique demands of the content and the needs of the class.

- Hashtag summaries can be used to garnish student feedback and opinions on a particular lesson or activity. For example, instead of using Hashtag summaries after a lesson, use them before introducing an activity. If your lesson centers around abstract art, have students reflect on their prior knowledge and/or misconceptions about what abstract art may be. You may get some funny ones, such as *#idontknowwhatiamlookingat*, *#weird*, *#shapesandthings*, or *#confusing*.

- Instead of using tweets as the method of response, have students use images from the lesson and create their own Instagram captions.

- Use Tweet Summaries as exit tickets or responses that summarize a lesson or ideas of the day. Because tweets are a fixed number of characters, students are forced to eliminate the fluff in their summaries and focus only on the key details. Additionally, because tweeting requires little writing, even reluctant students are more likely to take part in the activity.

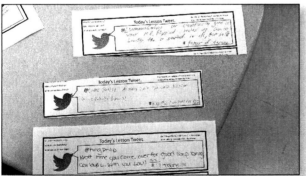 

☆ Above are Tweet Summaries used in a science classroom.

Extensions

- Use the tweets as starters for extended written responses.

- Match Instagram-type pictures and captions with tweets that address the same material.

- Challenge students to expand the tweets into Written Conversations (page 27) with classmates using tweets as the means of delivery.

Content-Area Crossover

- Social Studies—Have students create Social Media Summaries (tweets, hashtags, or Instagram captions) to summarize content learned. These summaries can happen before, during, or after a lesson to summarize chapter sections, primary-source documents, speeches, historical films, or photographs.

- Math—Have students create Social Media Summaries as responses to individual math problems or as exit tickets out of the class for the day.

- Science—Students could add Social Media Summaries as sections on lab reports. Have students create hypotheses and summarize them with hashtags or tweets. Conversely, when experiments are completed, have students conclude their reports with Social Media Summaries.

- Art—Use Social Media Summaries to describe movements in art or music, composers, or artists after teaching a unit. Social Media Summaries could also be used as preteaching strategies to gather what students know about a unit before introducing it.

Author's Thoughts

All of my students love these summaries. I often use sample tweets to have students predict what they think the lesson will be about. Sometimes I display sample tweets from a variety of people about the same topic. I then ask students to choose which of the tweets has the strongest summarizing statement about that event. I've even had students review a variety of tweets about a number of events and have students classify and sort them. I once used Social Media Summaries to have students research actual Twitter postings regarding an event to gather other people's opinions about current events. The ideas are endless.

Writing to Organize

Organization is one of the main components of writing that students have to master in order to be effective. In order to convey a message, whether written, spoken, or visually represented, it must be well organized and thought out. Poorly planned compositions often result in miscommunication and confusion simply because they lack effective organization. No matter what genre, format, content area, or discipline, if writing is meant to be effectively shared, displayed, or read by audiences, it must be well organized and clear.

Many studies have shown that teaching effective planning strategies that aid in organization of compositions yields significant positive effects (Graham 2006). Routman (2005, 13) lists the need to "present ideas clearly, with a logical, well-organized flow" as one of the 12 writing essentials for all grade levels.

The strategies in this section address this crucial component of writing. Each of the strategies offers opportunities to teach students how to organize their thoughts. The following strategies can be used as tools for organizing:

★ Four-Block Writing 86

★ Paint-Strip Organizer 89

★ Heard, Refute, and Question (HRQ) 91

★ List, Group, Label, and Map 93

★ Compare-and-Contrast Thrown Down 95

★ Mock Pinterest Pages 99

Four-Block Writing

Background

Four-Block Writing requires students to compartmentalize and organize information and assists in developing organized notes that can be used for extended writing or meaningful classroom discussions later.

Benefits

- This activity requires students to organize material for personal use later.

- This activity can be modified to fit a number of tasks.

- This activity organizes ideas and notes for extended writing pieces.

- Students practice note-taking skills.

- Students share and revisit key ideas.

Procedure

1. Have students fold papers into four quadrants or use the template on page 111.

2. Then, have students label each section with the topics you want them to address. Students should add notes (sketches, words, phrases, or sentences).

3. Have students add, delete, modify, or edit information for each section throughout the lesson/unit.

4. Have students share notes. This step can be completed as a class, with a partner, or in groups. Allow students an opportunity to share and add additional information based on ideas from their peers. **Note:** You can stop here if the objective was to take notes and elicit ideas for classroom discussion. If you want to extend the writing, continue with steps 5 and 6.

5. Once enough information has been collected, have students cut apart the four sections. Students can use each section to write about one topic or write a larger piece on all four topics.

6. Instruct students to display one block at a time. All other pieces of paper should be placed out of view. Once students finish writing about everything in one block, have them move on to another block until all four blocks are complete.

Modifications

- Don't have four topics that need to be covered? No problem. Fold the paper into two or three sections, and continue the activity as described.

- Have students draw pictorial representations of each category in addition to or as a substitute for the initial writing.

Extensions

- Use this activity to help students draft essays about the unit.

- Challenge students to create companion pictorial four-block organizers that can supplement the final product with illustrations that complement the composition.

Rock Star Tip

I found that if students kept the details for all of the paragraphs in front of them, they would be tempted to use them. By only displaying one block at a time, students are not tempted to merge ideas from one paragraph into another one.

People

George Washington

Samuel Adams

John Adams

John Hancock

Thomas Jefferson

Locations

Concord

Lexington

Boston

Philadelphia

Valley Forge

Cowpens

Yorktown

Materials

fabric

lead

lumber / wood

iron

guns

Symbols

freedom

flag

The Liberty Bell

☆ This organization writing activity was conducted in a social studies classroom.

Content-Area Crossover

- Social Studies—Use the Four-Block Writing Strategy as a way to research key historical figures, regions, areas, or specific laws, rules, or regulations that have been passed.

- Science—Use this strategy as an alternative to the traditional lab reports as a way to expand on topics that have multiple components, include figures or diagrams that complement the material, or to show something that involves a process. In science, you may include sections in a unit, and in physics you could include Newton's Second Law of Motion, velocity, energy conservation, and formulas and examples of this law.

- Math—Students may use the Four-Block Writing Strategy to include sections for linear, polynomial, quadratic, and rational functions. Try using the activity to assist students when solving complex problems. Teachers can amend the four-block labels to best suit the demands of the math task. Four sample labels could be:

  - What do I know?

  - What do I need to learn?

  - What is my strategy?

  - How do I know my answer is correct?

Author's Thoughts

Regardless of the subject or grade level, when I taught, the majority of my students struggled with organization. They specifically had a hard time structuring a paragraph so that everything in one paragraph related to one individual topic. Details that were off topic often managed to sneak into the paragraph. Do you have students like that? I'll bet you do.

To assist these learners I incorporated the Four-Block Writing activity into my lessons to teach students how to organize their writing. This addition served as a support for developing extended composition pieces.

Paint-Strip Organizer

Author's Thoughts

On a recent trip to an art museum, my social studies colleague used this activity to have students write about common themes, colors, and symbols prevalent in ancient Chinese art. Students filled in three complete paint strips, organizing themes, colors, and symbols that they observed during their trip. Later, this writing was used to aid classroom discussions. Each student was then assigned one of the blocks as a research assignment on the symbolic meanings behind imagery in ancient Chinese art.

Background

A key component of each writing-to-organize strategy often revolves around finding important information and organizing this information. In content-area classes, students sometimes have difficulty finding quality sources. They may need to tease out steps involved in an experiment or decipher credible (and reliable) sources for document-based questions (DBQs) in social studies. Because paint strips have individual blocks or compartments, they become fantastic vehicles for these kinds of tasks.

Content-area classroom teachers can use paint strips as places to organize this information or as ways of listing sequential steps. You will want to frontload this activity for students by telling them what types of information to pay attention to during the lesson, movie, trip, etc.

Benefits

- This activity requires students to be succinct and specific as they support their answers.

- Students have the opportunity to explore specific types of words and phrases (transition and Tier-Three/Level-Three words) that are often used in content-area writing.

Procedure

1. Determine the topic or concept that students will write about. **Note:** If you are frontloading this activity, tell students what types of information they need to locate or what topics they should take notes about.

2. Provide students with paint strips (or use the template on page 115). The number of blocks on each strip should correspond with the number of steps, details, and/or topics that should be listed by the completion of the activity.

3. Teach content-area material.

Modifications

- Use comic-strip templates instead of paint strips to achieve a similar effect.

- Students can alternate between writing texts on some of the spaces and drawing visual images on others.

Paint-Strip Organizer *(cont.)*

Extensions

- This activity can be used as a starting point for fully developed technical writing or procedural pieces.

- This activity can be used as a starting point for classroom discussions or partner conversations.

Content-Area Crossover

Any content-area classroom that requires students to organize, store, note, or review content can benefit from using the paint-strip strategy.

Each content-area class can modified this activity to reflect objectives to meet the needs of each individual student. This activity can be used for one lesson, stored and used as a living document, or used at the end of a lesson/unit to assess students' understanding of the content.

- Math—In the math class where students learn the orders of operation, use paint strips to demonstrate the sequencing of each step. A Paint-Strip Organizer may help students see what comes first, in the middle, and at the end of a rule like PEMDAS.

☆ This Paint-Strip organizer activity was conducted in science class. Students later used this draft as a longer writing assignment.

Heard, Refute, and Question (HRQ)

Background

The Heard, Refute, and Question (HRQ) strategy functions much like a KWL chart does. In a KWL chart, one column is for what you *Know*, one column is for what you *Want* to know, and one column is for what you *Learned*. In an HRQ chart, the *H* stands for what you have *Heard* about something, the *R* is what you can now *Refute* after some learning, and the *Q* stands for *Questions* you still have about the topic.

The magic of this activity is in the word *heard*. *Heard* is a low-stakes word. What you heard as opposed to something you 'know' is much less intimidating to students. In the past, when I asked students what they knew about something, many of them would say, "Nothing." The word *know* is a high-stakes word. In order to know something, it is assumed that what you know must be correct. For a many students, this absolute can be intimidating.

Benefits

- This activity activates prior knowledge.

- The activity is quick and can be completed before, during, or after a lesson unit.

- This activity encourages students to notice and correct their misconceptions.

Procedure

1. Direct students to create a three-column grid or use the HRQ template on page 109. Have students label the columns "H," "R," and "Q."

2. Discuss the expectations for all columns as they fit the lesson.

3. Have students fill in the *H* column.

4. After teaching some of the concept, return to the *H* column, and identify information students can now *refute*. This becomes the basis for the *R* column. **Note:** Students should look at every point in the *H* column and refute each of their misconceptions.

5. Have students fill in the *R* (Refute) column using evidence from classroom materials.

6. At the end of your unit/lesson, have students add any questions that they still have about the concept in the *Q* column.

Modification

- Try mixing and matching parts of the KWL with HRQ. For example, use a HWQ chart prior to a lesson, and ask students, *"What have you heard? What do you want to know? What questions do you still have?"* Or you may try HNL in the middle of a unit by asking students, *"What have you heard? What do you need to know? What have you learned?"* There are several different ways to modify this strategy. (See page 109 for the template.)

Extensions

- Use the HRQ activity as a springboard to constructing summaries about a unit once all the columns are complete.

- For topics that are pivotal in a subject area, add another column titled *E* for *examples*. Students can then list examples when they encounter them in their studies.

Content-Area Crossover

HRQs are flexible. This activity can easily be differentiated to fit the needs, demands, and tasks in the content-area classroom. If your objective is to see what students know, your chart will focus more on the *Heard* and *Refute* columns.

Likewise, if you want students to actively question the material, ideas, and topics taught, you will include the *Question* and *Want* columns. If you use this activity as a culminating activity or an assessment, make sure to include the *Know* and *Learned* columns.

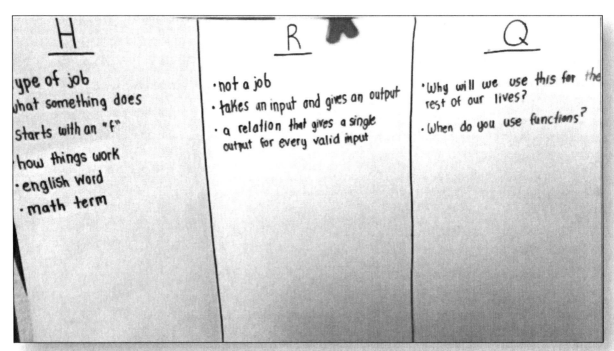

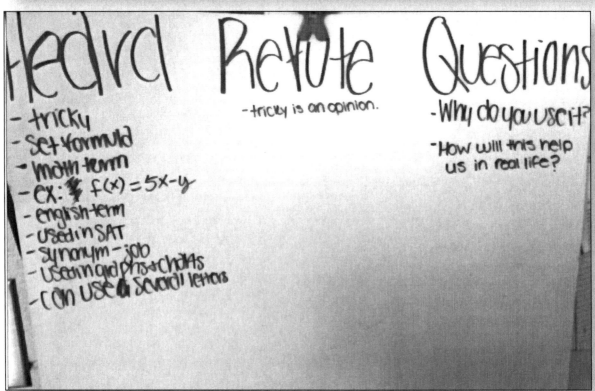

☆ Here are two variations of the Heard, Refute, and Question activity.

List, Group, Label, and Map

Background

List, Group, Label, and Map is an effective strategy for activating prior knowledge, brainstorming, thinking about concept-specific vocabulary, and organizing all these components. This activity also capitalizes on the writing-to-learn principles because much of the writing stays in the initial stages (The WAC Clearinghouse 2016). You can use as many of the components as the lesson warrants. In addition, this activity can be picked up, paused, and resumed at times that best fit the lesson. This amount of flexibility makes it easy to implement in any content-area classroom.

List, Group, Label, and Map starts as a low-stakes writing assignment—a list—and then uses the words generated in the list for grouping into categories that can be labeled and mapped onto a concept map. Because it begins with an informal list, it is easier to tackle than a blank concept/bubble map where students have to predetermine what categories should be included. In this manner the groups/categories emerge in a more organic nature and are shaped into concept maps that are unique to each individual lesson.

Benefits

- This activity is flexible. It can be used at the beginning, in the middle, or as a review at the end of a unit.

- This activity requires students to synthesize information.

- This activity encourages creative divergent thinking.

- This activity is quick and can easily be integrates into any lesson.

Procedure

1. Introduce a concept. **Note:** Make sure students have adequate background knowledge before beginning the activity.(Use one of the evidence activities from the *Writing to Prove* section).

2. Have students *list* all the words they know about the topic on note cards with one word or short phrase per card. This list can be individual or displayed as a class list.

3. Have students *group* the words from their lists into piles based on common attributes. **Note:** If you are using this activity with a whole class, divide students into groups, and have them select several words to group.

4. Have students select a *label* to describe each group.

5. Then, have students transfer their groups and labels to cluster maps.

Modification

- Do you have multiple student groups? Have students from one class use the words brainstormed by another.

Extensions

- For the map, you can have students transfer the material onto cluster-map graphic organizers or have them simply paste their note cards on large sheets of chart paper in cluster-map format.

- Have students use the material from the maps to construct responses about the concept from questions posed in class.

- If there are leftover words from the first phase of the activity, use them as tickets in the door and have students place them on the correct maps as they enter the class.

Rock Star Tip

If you want to avoid numerous repeated words, have students display their words one at a time with the explicit instruction not to replicate. Or you may assign this activity as a group. Have each group write multiple words so, if their word is taken, they have a bank of other words to choose from.

Content-Area Crossover

All content-area classrooms can capitalize on this type of writing. Because the stakes are lower than traditional essay writing, reluctant writers are likely to be successful when completing this activity. Each content-area classroom should modify the demands and objectives; making sure they are suitable for each lesson and task.

Additionally, this activity can be used in part or as a whole, depending on your classroom needs. If you want students to think and generate ideas about a topic, you can only conduct the first two steps in this activity (*list* and *group*). If you want finished published essays, you will want to complete each step (*list*, *group*, *label*, and *map*).

> ### Rock Star Tip
>
> Mapping this way arrives and emerges in a more organic nature; the organization is created during the process. Traditional cluster maps require students to have ideas of their main topics and subtopics. What if students don't know enough about the topic to be able to discuss the subtopics? If this is the case, then creating cluster maps in that manner is difficult. However, if students start with lists or another low-stakes writing assignment and then use the lists of words to group, label, and map, the cluster maps become much easier.

☆ These are the first steps (*list* and *group*) of the List, Group, Label, and Map activity.

Compare-and-Contrast Throw Down

Background

The skills of sorting, analyzing, and comparing are forms of organization. Students must organize their thoughts and focus on similarities and differences. One effective way for teachers to address comparing is with the Compare-and-Contrast Throw Down. Instead of having students organize information on paper or graphic organizers, allow them to walk around the classroom and interact with classmates to achieve the same results.

For this activity, students throw down words and/or phrases for each concept in a pile. These categories can be used for extended classroom discussions, projects, or for writing later. (**Note:** Pay close attention to the word "throw." Students love it. It makes the whole activity much more fun.)

Benefits

- This is a low-stakes activity.

- This activity aids in sentence and paragraph construction.

- This activity aids in vocabulary acquisition.

- Students are required to be succinct and specific since they are limited by writing space.

Procedure

1. Determine what concepts students will compare.

2. Ask students to consider the first concept.

3. Give students note cards, and have them write something about the concept and throw the card on the ground in the designated spot.

Author's Thoughts

One of the best introductions to this strategy is through the use of media. I use movie trailers when I teach comparing as a skill. Prior to the activity, I label cards *Original* and *Remake*.

For my initial lesson, I start with the original trailer for a movie. We watch the brief trailer, and then students write what they noticed on note cards. After they record their observations, students come to the floor and throw their cards on the floor near the labels. We then watch a trailer for the remake of the movie and repeat the activity.

After this, we watch each trailer once more. This time, students use their note cards to write what the trailers have in common. These are placed on the floor next to the *Both* label. At this point, there are now tons of words that describe each trailer individually and words that describe their common attributes.

4. Repeat this process for the other concept(s) and the attributes the concepts share. **Note:** Once this is done, you can stop the activity and sum it up with a discussion reviewing some of the cards in each pile or proceed to steps 5 and 6.

5. Have students pick up one word from each pile on the floor. **Note:** If students select words that do not fit in the category, no problem—have an exchange policy so students can swap their note cards.

6. Students should use their chosen words to write one sentence about each concept and a third sentence about their common attributes.

Modifications

- If you have more than two items to compare, make sure to include space on the floor or wall to compare and contrast multiple concepts.

- Consider color-coding the cards so students do not forget which pile each card came from.

- If you have only one concept to discuss, students can throw down characteristics or traits relating to that one concept.

- Worried that the piles of words will get out of control? Use a plastic hoop to contain the words. What you end up with is a 3-D Venn diagram.

☆ Students search for similarities and differences during Compare-and-Contrast Throw Down.

51560—Content-Area Writing That Rocks (and Works!)   © Shell Education

Compare-and-Contrast Throw Down *(cont.)*

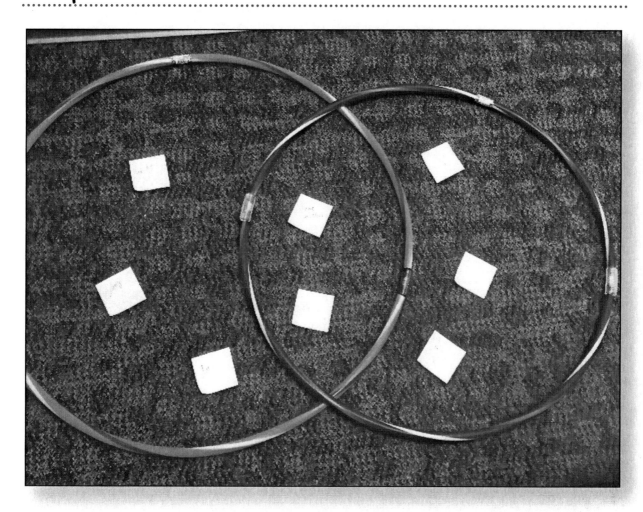

☆ Use plastic hoops to help contain the cards that students throw down during Compare-and-Contrast Throw Down.

Extensions

- Continue this activity by having students go back to get more words until they have written several sentences.

- Extend the sentence writing into a paragraph or an essay.

- At the end of this activity, if students are expected to write extended pieces, I typically give them three new note cards and tell them to transfer sentences that compare, contrast, and do both to three different note cards. Essentially, students have created three paragraphs comparing these concepts.

- Encourage students to work on listening and speaking standards by choosing words from each pile and discussing ideas.

- If you are using this activity coupled with text, have students use three different-color highlighters to highlight the sentences. Have them highlight one concept sentence in one color, the second concept sentence in another color, and the sentence about both in a third color.

Content-Area Crossover

Any classroom that requires students to compare, analyze, or synthesize content can utilize this activity. Modify the lesson based on your task objectives and the developmental demands of your students. This activity can be coupled with the Continuum Debate on page 51 to foster classroom discussions and deepen understanding of content.

Drumming for More

There are tons of trailers on YouTube that you can use to model this activity. Roald Dahl and Disney movies are always favorites of mine since many of these original movies have been remade.

☆ In a social studies classroom, students compare and contrast Thurgood Marshall and Frederick Douglass.

Mock Pinterest Pages

Background

Some students are visual learners and need activities in school to tap into this for academic success. Even if your students are not visual learners, many of them may benefit from the opportunity to experience concepts through visual representations. Visuals help cement concepts that are abstract or foreign to students.

So, what does Pinterest have to do with all this? Having images included with instructions or descriptions makes concepts more convincing, real, and authentic. For some reason, recipes come alive, hairstyles jump off the page, and home décor ideas seem attainable when images accompany directions.

Another unique component of this site is the organizational aspect of the Pinterest boards. With Pinterest, users organize all items that go together with certain themes. While users can name their own boards to suit their style, the site also groups posts according to categories, which helps novice organizers. Pinterest appeals to individuals' needs for visual representation as well as compartmentalization of concepts into neat, organized groups. It allows individuals to choose items and subjects that appeal specifically to their interests.

☆ Here are two Mock Pinterest Pages that students created after completing a fable and fairy tale unit.

Benefits

- This activity requires students to practice research.

- This activity encourages students to think critically about a subject.

- Students are able to represent concepts with text and visual images.

- Students practice categorizing and grouping information by commonalities.

- This activity will interest visual learners.

Procedure

1. Provide students with a visual example of a Pinterest page. **Note:** If you want students to create digital pages, model how to do this. If you prefer hard copy, model the finished product for students.

2. Provide students a list of potential topics to choose from.

3. Explain how many boards and images and how much other information should be included.

Modification

- This particular activity could be completed by individual students, with partners, or in groups, depending on the constraints of the classroom.

Extensions

- Have students complete a written justification for each board or image included.

- Use a rubric or a checklist to focus students' entries and assess students' Pinterest pages.

- Compile multiple boards into a portfolio of a concept as a culminating activity.

- When researching a historical figure, students will have to research the figure's past to determine the types of items that the person would pin on his or her board. Have students determine which other historical figures their individual would follow on Pinterest.

Content-Area Crossover

- Social Studies—You can assign students a historical figure, a political party, or a geographic region to research. Your culminating research project may include a variety of smaller boards/pages that the individual student or group might "pin."

- Math—Math teachers may use this activity for large units of study that include a large amount of information, such as linear functions.

- Science—Science teachers may have students create Mock Pinterest Pages for elements on the periodic table. Information about the elements' natural states, everyday uses, atomic number, and makeup could be included.

- Art—Art teachers may find that this is a natural strategy for studying specific works of art or art movements because of the visual nature of the activity.

Rock Star Tip

Want to try a digital version? Try Glogster (edu.glogster.com), a multimedia Internet poster application that allows users to create a digital version of a bulletin board or a poster.

Letter from the Author

To all my Rock Star Content-Area Teachers,

For me, the teaching of writing in all content areas and at all times is something that I embrace and love. While I understand that integrating content literacy, especially the task of writing, in all content areas, can be challenging, it is one that I welcome. This is mainly because I am intrigued by the methods in which people use writing as a communicative vehicle. I am the one who asks random students what they are writing and reading, the one who notices the types of writing everyday people do, and makes random notes about ways that writing can be taught and enhanced through unique methods of instruction.

My hope is that through this book, you have found ideas and strategies that work well with what you are charged with teaching. While it would be naive to assume that everyone could use everything I have included here, my end goal is for content-area teachers to pick up this book and find strategies that can enhance, assist, and in some ways, change the way you view writing in your class. If a strategy doesn't jive with you, skip it…for now. Sometimes you are down the road when you find that the idea you read about months ago is now the perfect solution to a need in the classroom.

Thanks for sharing this time together,

Rock on!

Rebecca G. Harper

References Cited

Allen, Janet. 2000. *Yellow Brick Roads: Shared and Guided Paths to Independent Reading 4–12*. Portland, ME. Stenhouse Publishers.

Baker S. K., Deborah C. Simmons, and Edward J. Kame'enui. 1995. Vocabulary Acquisition: Synthesis of the Research. National Center to Improve the Tools of Education Technical Report 13.

Bandura, Albert. 1977. *Social Learning Theory*. Englewood Cliffs, NJ: Prentice Hall.

Beck, Isabel L., Margaret G. McKeown, and Linda Kucan. 2002. *Bringing Words to Life*. New York: Guilford Press.

Berke, J., and R. Woodland. 1995. Twenty Questions for the Writer: A Rhetoric with Readings (6th ed.). Fort Worth, TX: Harcourt Brace College Publishers.

Berninger, V. W., and H. L. Swanson. 1994. "Modification of the Hayes and Flower Model to Explain Beginning and Developing Writing." Advances in Cognition and Educational Practice 2: *Children's Writing: Toward a Process Theory of Development of Skilled Writing*. Greenwich, CT. 57–82.

Bruner, J. 1990. Acts of Meaning. Cambridge, MA: Harvard University Press.

Combs, Warren E. 2012. Writer's Workshop for Common Core: A Step-by-Step Guide. Larchmont, NY: Eye on Education.

Compton-Lilly, C. 2004. Confronting Racism, Poverty, and Power: Classroom Strategies to Change the World. Portsmouth: Heinemann.

Connelly, F. M., and D. J. Clandinin. 1990. "Stories of Experience and Narrative Inquiry." Educational Research 19: 2–14.

Cook-Gumperz, J. 1986. The Social Construction of Literacy. Cambridge, England: Cambridge University Press.

Daniels, Harvey, Steven Zemelman, and Nancy Steineke. 2007. Content-Area Writing: Every Teacher's Guide. Portsmouth: Heinemann.

Dantas, M. L., and P. C. Manyak (Eds.). 2010. Home-School Connections in a Multicultural Society: Learning from and with Culturally and Linguistically Diverse Families. New York: Routledge.

Denman, G. A. 1991. Sit Tight and I'll Swing You a Tail: Using and Writing Stories with Young People. Portsmouth: Heinemann.

Dewey, J. (1916). Democracy and Education. New York, NY: The Macmillan Company.

Dyson, A. H., and C. Genishi. 1994. The Need for Story: Cultural Diversity in Classroom and Community. Urbana: National Council of Teachers of English.

Ellis, A. 1985. "The Cognitive Neuropsychology of Developmental (and Acquired) Dyslexia: A Critical Survey." Cognitive Neuropsychology 2: 169–205.

———. 1987. "Review on Problems in Developing Cognitively Transmitted Cognitive Models." Mind and Language 2: 242–251.

Flower, L., and J. R. Hayes. 1981. "A Cognitive Process Theory of Writing." College Composition and Communication 32(4): 365–387.

Gadsden, V. 1998. "Family Cultures and Literacy Learning." *Literacy for All: Issues in Teaching and Learning.* New York: Guilford Press.

———. 1999. "Black Families in Intergenerational and Cultural Perspective." *Families, Parenting and Child Development in "Nontraditional."* (221–246).

Gee, J. P. 1989. "What Is Literacy?" *Journal of Education,* 171 (1): 18–25.

Graham. S. 2006. "Strategy Instruction and the Teaching of Writing: A Meta-Analysis." *Handbook of Writing Research.* New York: Guilford.

Harvey, Stephanie. 1998. *Nonfiction Matters: Reading, Writing, and Research in Grades 3–8.* Portland, ME: Stenhouse Publishers.

Hilden, Katherine, and Jennifer Jones. 2012. "A Literacy Spring Cleaning: Sweeping Round Robin Reading Out of Your Classroom." *Reading Today* 29 (5): 23–24.

Hollie, Sharroky. 2012. Culturally and Linguistically Responsive Teaching and Learning. Huntington Beach, CA: Shell Education.

Hyde. Arthur. 2006. *Comprehending Math: Adapting Reading Strategies to Teach Mathematics, K–6.* Portsmouth, NH: Heinmann.

Kress, Gunther, and Theo van Leeuwen. 1996. Reading Images: The Grammar of Visual Design. New York: Routledge.

Langer, Judith A. 1984. "Examining Background Knowledge and Text Comprehension." *Reading Research Quarterly* 19 (4): 468–481.

Langer, Judith A., and Arthur N. Applebee. 1987. How Writing Shapes Thinking. National Council of Teachers.

Lankshear, C., and M. Knobel. 1998. F. Christie and R. Misson (Eds.). Literacy and Schooling. London: Routledge. 155–177.

Maxwell, Martha J. 1966. "Training College Reading Specialists." *Journal of Reading* 10 (3): 147–155.

McCutchen, D. 2000. "Knowledge Acquisition, Processing Efficiency, and Working Memory: Implications for a Theory of Writing." *Educational Psychologist* 35: 13–23.

McKenna, M. C., R. D. Robinson. 1990. "Content Literacy: A Definition and Implications." *Journal of Reading.* 34 (3): 167.

Moll, L., C. Amanti, D. Neff, and N. Gonzalez. 1992. "Funds of Knowledge for Teaching: Using a Qualitative Approach to Connect Homes and Classrooms." *Theory into Practice*, 31(2), 132–141.

National Commission on Writing for America's Schools and Colleges. 2004. Writing: A Ticket to Work… Or a Ticket Out. National Writing Project.

National Council of Social Studies. 2015. "Improving Historical Reading and Writing." http://www .socialstudies.org.

National Council of Teachers of Mathematics. 2000. Principles and Standards for School Mathematics. Reston: The National Council of Teachers of Mathematics, Inc.

National Institute for Literacy. 2010. *What Content-Area Teachers Know about Adolescent Literacy.* Eunice Kennedy Shriver National Institute of Child Health. Washington, D.C.: U.S. Government Printing Office.

National Science Teachers Association. 2013. Next Generation Science Standards. http://www.nsta .org.

National Writing Project. 2016. http://www.nwp.org.

National Writing Project and Nagin, C. 2006. Because Writing Matters: Improving Student Writing in Our Schools. San Francisco: Jossey-Bass.

Newell, G. E., and P. Winograd. 1995. "Writing about and Learning from History Texts: The Effects of Task and Academic Ability." Research in the Teaching of English 29: 133–163.

Next Generation Science Standards. 2013. "Appendix M—Connections to the Common Core State Standards for Literacy in Science and Technical Subjects." http://www.nextgenscience.org.

Park, Jie Y. 2012. "A Different Kind of Reading Instruction: Using Visualization to Bridge Reading Comprehension and Critical Literacy." Journal of Adolescent & Adult Literacy 55 (7): 629–640.

Probst, R. E. 1988. "Dialogue with a Text." The English Journal, Vol. 77 (1): 32–38.

Rosenblatt, L. M. 1994. The Reader, the Text, the Poem. Carbondale: Southern Illinois University Press.

Routman, R. 2005. *Writing Essentials: Reading Expectations and Results while Simplifying Teaching.* Portsmouth, NH: Heinemann.

Swanson, H. L., and V. W. Berninger. 1996. "Individual Differences in Children's Working Memory and Writing Skills." Journal of Experimental Child Psychology 63 (2).

Taylor, D. (Ed.). 1997. *Many Families, Many Literacies: An International Declaration of Principles.* Portsmouth, NH: Heinemann.

The WAC Clearing House. 2016. https://wac.colostate.edu.

Young, I. 2000. Inclusion and Democracy. New York: Oxford University Press.

Name:_____ Date: _____

School-Based Interest Inventory

Directions: Getting to know you is important. Answer each question about your interests.

What is your favorite class or activity in school?

_____

_____

What is your least favorite class or activity in school?

_____

_____

Who are your favorite teachers? Why?

_____

_____

Describe your favorite subject in school.

_____

_____

What could be better about your time in school?

_____

_____

Do you like working alone, in small groups, or in large groups?

_____

_____

What do you plan on doing once you are done with school?

_____

_____

How would you describe a good student?

_____

_____

Name:_____ Date: _____

Extracurricular Activities Interest Inventory

Directions: Getting to know you is important. Answer each question about your interests.

What do you do in your spare time?

_____

_____

Do you use social media? If so, which sites?

_____

_____

How much time each day do you spend using technology? (smartphones, computers, etc.)

_____

_____

Do you have any responsibilities outside of school? (job, watching siblings, chores, etc.)

_____

_____

Do you belong to any clubs or teams at school?

_____

_____

Do you take part in any extracurricular activities outside school? (clubs, community groups)

_____

_____

Which activities would you like to participate in outside of school? Why?

_____

_____

Name:_____ Date: _____

General Interest Inventory

Directions: Getting to know you is important. Answer each question about your interests.

Describe yourself in three words.

_____

_____

What is your favorite television show or movie? Why?

_____

_____

What type of music do you listen to? Why?

_____

_____

Describe a time when you felt proud of yourself.

_____

_____

What is your favorite food?

_____

_____

What is your best quality or the best thing about you?

_____

_____

Do you have any special talents? If so, what are they?

_____

_____

Do you have pets? If so, what kind?

_____

_____

Name:_____ Date: _____

Alpha-Boxes Template

Directions: Write the topic above the chart, and then brainstorm as many words as you can related to the topic. Add the words to the boxes with the letter that begins the words.

For example: Epic would go in the E box.

_____

A	B	C	D	E
F	**G**	**H**	**I**	**J**
K	**L**	**M**	**N**	**O**
P	**Q**	**R**	**S**	**T**
U	**V**	**W**	**XYZ**	

Name:_____ Date: _____

HRQ Template

Directions: Select one label to place at the top of each column.

> **H** (heard)—What have you heard?
>
> **R** (refute)—What information can you refute from the previous column?
>
> **Q** (question)—What questions do you have about the topic?
>
> **W** (want)—What do you want to know about the topic?
>
> **N** (need)—What information do you need to know about the topic?
>
> **L** (learned)—What information did you learn about the topic?

Name:_____ Date: _____

Bio Poem 2.0 Template

Directions: Complete each line using information about your chosen topic. Be specific.

Line 1: Your character/historical figure's name or name of concept

Line 2: Four words that describe your person or concept

Line 3: Brother or sister of

Line 4: Lover of (list three ideas, people, or concepts)

Line 5: Who feels (three examples)

Line 6: Who needs (three examples)

Line 7: Who gives (three examples)

Line 8: Who fears (three examples)

Line 9: Who would like to see

Line 10: Resident of

Line 11: Your character/historical figure's name or name of concept

1. _____

2. _____ _____ _____ _____

3. _____

4. _____ _____ _____

5. _____ _____ _____

6. _____ _____ _____

7. _____ _____ _____

8. _____ _____ _____

9. _____

10. _____

11. _____

Name:_____ Date: _____

Four-Block Writing Template

Directions: Select four categories, and insert one label at the top of each cell.

Common labels are *materials, people, locations, symbols,* and *topics*.

_____

_____

_____

_____

Name:_____ Date: _____

Red-Light, Green-Light Evidence Template

Directions: Use the organizer to sort your evidence into three categories.

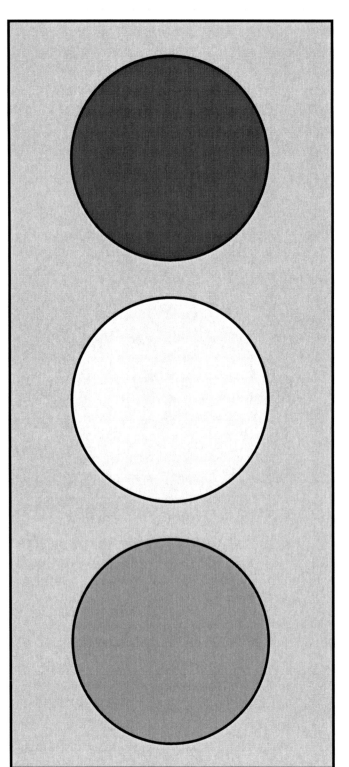

Red: Information that is off topic.

Yellow: Information that you are unsure of.

Green: Information that you are sure about.

       © *Shell Education*

Name:_____ Date: _____

Levels of Words Template

Directions: Record words in the chart according to their levels.

> Make sure to check with your teacher to determine how you are sorting the words.

Level-Three Words

Level-Two Words

Level-One Words

Name:_____ Date: _____

Do This, Not That Recipe Template

Directions: Use the template below to make a recipe card for your selected topic.

> **Note:** Make sure to use credible sources when researching to complete this activity.

Title of Topic:	Image of Concept Being Studied:
Information:	Other Facts:

Why the Topic Is Better than the Alternative:

    © *Shell Education*

Name:_____ Date: _____

Paint-Strip Template

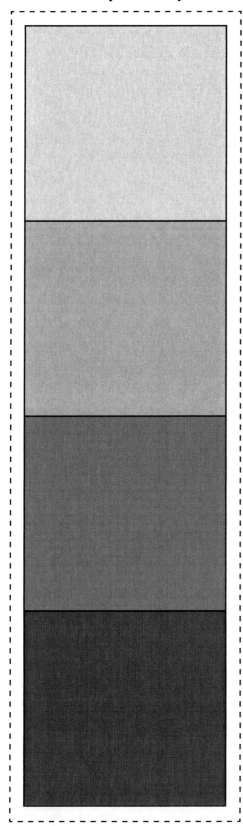
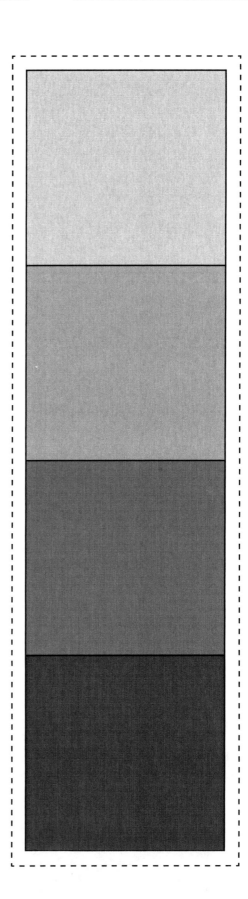

Name:_____ Date: _____

Social Media Summaries Template

Directions: Use the social media templates below to write a summary. Remember, if you are completing a tweet summary, you can only use 140 characters.

  © *Shell Education*

Name:_____ Date: _____

iPod List Template

Directions: Use the iPod template to create a playlist. Explain each song entry on the lines below.

_____

_____

_____

_____

_____

Books That Rock!

Over the years, I have collected a variety of books that I incorporate in my content-literacy classes. These books appeal to students because they are engaging, relevant, and relatable. Many of the books listed are those I stumbled upon by accident that later became staples in my classrooms. Here is a sample of my favorites.

Math

Spaghetti and Meatballs for All by Marilyn Burns

The Number Devil: A Mathematical Adventure by Hans Magnus Enzensberger

An Abundance of Katherines by John Green

Secrets, Lies, and Algebra by Wendy Lichtman

G is for Googol: A Math Alphabet Book by David M. Schwartz

Math Curse by John Scieszka and Lane Smith

365 Penguins by Jean-Luc Fromental

Brown Bear, Brown Bear, What Do You See? by Bill Martin Jr. and Eric Carle

Science

I Feel Better With a Frog in My Throat: History's Strangest Cures by Carlyn Beccia

How They Croaked: The Awful Ends of the Awfully Famous by Georgia Bragg

How They Choked: Failures, Flops, and Flaws of the Awfully Famous by Georgia Bragg

Who Would Win? series by Jerry Pallotta (They're all fantastic!)

Q is for Quark: A Science Alphabet Book by David M. Schwartz

Tadpole's Promise by Jeanne Willis and Tony Ross

The Very Hungry Caterpillar by Eric Carle

Books That Rock! *(cont.)*

Social Studies

14 Cows for America by Carmen Agra Deedy

The Story of the H. L. Hunley and Queenie's Coin by Fran Hawk

Ick! Yuck! Eew! Our Gross American History by Lois Miner Huey

John, Paul, George, and Ben by Lane Smith

The Other Side by Jacqueline Woodson

The Mary Celeste: An Unsolved Mystery from History by Jane Yolen

Aunt Harriet's Underground Railroad in the Sky by Faith Ringgold

The Story of Ruby Bridges by Robert Coles and George Ford

ELA

The Crossover by Kwame Alexander

Out of My Mind by Sharon M. Draper

The Fourteenth Goldfish by Jennifer L. Holm

Fish in a Tree by Lynda Mullaly Hunt

Memoirs of a Goldfish by Devin Scillian

Memoirs of a Hamster by Devin Scillian

Counting By 7s by Holly Goldberg Sloan

The Giving Tree by Shel Silverstein

Where the Wild Things Are by Maurice Sendak

Notes

 　　　　　　　　© Shell Education